A History of Forest Entomology in the Intermountain and Rocky Mountain Areas, 1901 to 1982

By Malcolm M. Furniss

I0410824

United States Department of Agriculture / Forest Service
Rocky Mountain Research Station

General Technical Report RMRS-GTR-195
July 2007

Furniss, Malcolm M. 2007. **A history of forest entomology in the Intermountain and Rocky Mountain areas, 1901 to 1982**. Gen. Tech. Rep. RMRS-GTR-195. Fort Collins, CO: U.S. Department of Agriculture, Forest Service, Rocky Mountain Research Station. 40 p.

Abstract

This account spans the time from A.D. Hopkins' trip to the Black Hills, SD, in 1901 to my retirement in 1982. The focus is on personnel and the work of the Division of Forest Insect Investigations, USDA, and the Forest Service experiment stations in the Rocky Mountain and Intermountain areas. Information for the Intermountain and Northern Rocky Mountain station areas is derived from my experience there and as chairman of the history committee of the Western Forest Insect Work Conference (WFIWC). Information on the Rocky Mountain and Southwestern station areas came primarily from the WFIWC archives, University of Idaho, and from retired forest entomologists.

Keywords: Forest entomology, history, Rocky Mountain, Intermountain

Author

Malcolm M. Furniss was attracted to the outdoors while growing up in the Appalachian Mountains of rural New York State. In 1950, he graduated in forestry at the University of California and worked in California with the USDA Division of Forest Insect Investigations until transferring to the (Intermountain) INT station in 1954. He studied entomology at the University of Idaho and was Principal Research Entomologist and Project Leader at the Forestry Sciences Laboratory, Moscow, ID until retiring in 1982. He has studied bark beetles and other forest insects throughout western North America about which he has published over 100 articles.

Contents

Preface

This account is based in part on my experience during employment with the Division of Forest Insect Investigations, Bureau of Entomology and Plant Quarantine, USDA (1950 to 1953) and Forest Service, USDA, (1954 to 1982). Other sources of information were publications by A.D. Hopkins (Hopkins 1902, 1905, 1906), Harry Burke's recollections (Burke 1946), and Noel Wygant's oral history interview (Larson 1979a). These were supplemented by historical documents and photos in the Western Forest Insect Work Conference archives, recollections of others credited in the Acknowledgments, and my publications (Furniss 1997, 2003, 2004).

The focus of this account is on personnel and the work of the Division of Forest Insect Investigations (disbanded and transferred to the Forest Service in 1953) and the Forest Service Experiment Stations in the area concerned after 1953. The time period of my account spans the trip by Hopkins to the Black Hills, SD, in 1901, to the time of my retirement from the Forest Service in 1982; however, some recollections by Schmid and Mata (Appendix) extend beyond 1982 because they retired later.

Recollections of people in the Appendix and elsewhere, such as Noel Wygant's oral history interview (see Fort Collins Laboratory), are edited only lightly and passages referenced to my publications are as they appeared therein. This was done to preserve their integrity and the individual manner of expression — which throughout this paper is intended to be conversational and anecdotal. Consequently, some variation in style and grammar has resulted. The content of this paper is my responsibility alone and does not imply approval of the publisher.

Acknowledgments

The manuscript was reviewed by Gene Amman, INT (retired), Ogden, UT; David G. Fellin, INT (retired), Missoula, MT; Dennis E. Ferguson, Project Leader, RMRS, Moscow, ID; Melvin E. McKnight, RM (retired), Plainfield, VT; and John M. Schmid, RM (retired), Fort Collins, CO. Recollections of RM retirees were provided by Daniel T. Jennings, RM (retired), Garland, ME; Fred B. Knight, RM (retired), Holden, ME; Stephen A. Mata, RMRS (retired); William F. McCambridge, RM (deceased); McKnight; Schmid; and Robert E. Stevens, RM (retired), Jacksonville, OR. Sources of photos are identified in the figure captions. José Negron, RMRS, Fort Collins, CO, provided access to photographs taken by forest entomologists stationed in Fort Collins. Dennis Ferguson, RMRS, Moscow, ID, assisted with administrative aspects and without his help, this account could not have been published.

A History of Forest Entomology in the Intermountain and Rocky Mountain Areas, 1901 to 1982

By Malcolm M. Furniss

Introduction

Up to the time of Gifford Pinchot's appointment as head of the Division of Forestry in 1898, and continuing until 1905, public forests were under the jurisdiction of the Department of Interior's General Land Office, an agency that, according to Pinchot, was "incompetent to deal with the preservation of forests but it understood too little about forestry to know that it was incompetent." As he recalled later, "With our little force it was out of the question to do more than make a start on the forty-odd million acres of Forest Reserves (that had been established in 1893). But that start must not be delayed" (Furniss 1997).

Pinchot was receiving reports of bark beetle depredations from throughout the country. Neither his staff nor the new Division of Entomology, USDA, had an expert in forest entomology. The problem was solved by appointing Andrew Delmar Hopkins (fig. 1) of West Virginia University as a collaborator to conduct special investigations. Hopkins' first assignment was to investigate forest insect problems in the Pacific Northwest in 1899. In 1901, he went to the Black Hills, SD, at Pinchot's request to determine the cause of extensive pine mortality thought to be due to bark beetles (Burke 1946, Furniss 1997).

Andrew Delmar Hopkins (1857-1948)

The chain of events preceding Hopkins' appointment as a collaborator in 1899 had begun at the start of the decade. The newly created Agricultural Experiment Station at West Virginia University was looking for a state entomologist. Hopkins, whose formal education was restricted to the county schools of West Virginia, had taken over his grandfather's farm at age 17. Now at age 33,

he was about to embark on an unlikely and influential career. Through his characteristic persistence—perhaps enhanced by his offer to work for $1.00 per day to prove his worth—Hopkins was hired on 1 March 1890 for $50 per month "on trial" (Berisford 1991).

In order to get acquainted with the state's insect problems, he traveled extensively that summer and discovered a vast forest of bark beetle-killed spruce trees surrounding White Top Mountain in Randolph County (Hopkins 1891). The insect turned out to be the southern pine beetle, a member of the destructive bark beetle genus *Dendroctonus*, about which Hopkins was destined to become the world authority. His ensuing work on the

Figure 1. Andrew Delmar Hopkins, Chief of Forest Insect Investigations, Washington, D.C. Photo dated March 1909, the year that Josef Brunner was hired, marking the beginning of forest entomology in the northern Rocky Mountains (Bureau of Entomology photo 17310).

USDA Forest Service Gen. Tech. Rep. RMRS-GTR-195. 2007

1

southern pine beetle resulted in the University granting him an honorary Ph.D. degree in 1893, just 3 years after dropping farm work. Although Hopkins did brilliant work on many insects important to agriculture, his prominence as an expert on bark beetles would soon shape his future and that of American forest entomology.

Influenced by Pinchot, the USDA, Bureau of Entomology[1] created the Division of Forest Insect Investigations in 1902 and appointed Hopkins as head. In that era, the insects responsible for depredations being encountered in American forests were mostly unknown and not described. He set about changing that situation by specializing in bark beetles and hiring and training field personnel.

This account begins with Hopkins' visit to the Black Hills in 1901 in response to Pinchot's concern over extensive ponderosa pine mortality (Furniss 1997). The cause was found to be an unknown bark beetle, subsequently described as *Dendroctonus ponderosae* (Hopkins 1902) and given the common name Black Hills beetle[2]. From there, the story extends to Colorado where the same beetle and others caused concern in 1905 (Hopkins 1905), and to Montana in the northern Rocky Mountains where Hopkins employed Josef Brunner in 1909 (Furniss 2003). In time, Forest Insect Laboratories were established at Coeur d'Alene, ID (1919), Fort Collins, CO (1939), Ogden, UT (1949), and Albuquerque, NM (1952). The Bureau of Entomology and Plant Quarantine was disbanded in December, 1953, after which the personnel and mission of the Division of Forest Insect Investigations were transferred to the research branch (experiment stations) of the Forest Service.

---

[1] Herein, INT refers to the Intermountain Forest and Range Experiment Station and RM refers to the Rocky Mountain Forest and Range Experiment Station. The INT station was authorized in 1928 and created in 1930 (Klade 2006). In 1952, the Northern Rocky Mountain Forest and Range Experiment Station (NRM) that had been created in 1926 was joined under INT with headquarters in Ogden, UT. The RM station was created in 1935 (Price 1976). In 1953, the Southwestern Forest and Range Experiment Station (SW) that had been created in 1930 was joined under the RM station. In 1997, the INT station was joined with the RM station and the combined entity renamed the Rocky Mountain Research Station (RMRS) with headquarters in Fort Collins, CO (Klade 2006).

[2] As a result of synonymy of *D. ponderosae* and *D. monticolae* by S. L. Wood (1963), the common name "Black Hills beetle" was changed to "mountain pine beetle," The two names are used in this account interchangeably in the respective time periods.

Bark Beetle Depredations in the Black Hills — 1901

In 1897, Gifford Pinchot handed Special Forestry Expert Henry S. Graves (later Chief Forester, USDA Forest Service) the daunting assignment of measuring and describing the stands of forest trees on the 60,000 sq. mile, newly created Black Hills Forest Reserve. Along the way, Graves noted patches of dying pines on the high limestone divide in the North Hills and found an unknown bark beetle in all of them (Furniss 1997).

The tree killing increased and Hopkins was dispatched to the Black Hills in October, 1901, to look into the cause of the "depredations" (fig. 2). Hopkins confirmed that the trouble was caused by a bark beetle and named it *Dendroctonus ponderosae* (Hopkins 1902), known by the common name, Black Hills beetle. The type locality is Piedmont, SD. Today it is known as the mountain pine beetle and it infests several pine species over a large geographic area.

After Hopkins became head of the newly created USDA Division of Forest Insect Investigations in 1902, his first employee was Jesse L. Webb. Webb, a 1900 graduate of Washington State College, had studied forest entomology

Figure 2. Andrew D. Hopkins, far right, in the Black Hills in July 1902. From left are his employee, Jack Webb, Pathologist Dr. Hermann Von Schrank, and his assistant, Burns (Burke 1946).

under Hopkins at West Virginia University (MS 1902). He became the first college-trained forest entomologist in America. Webb was stationed at Elmore, SD, under direction of Hopkins, to study the beetle's seasonal history, predators and other associated insects, and to experiment with trap trees for control.

Trap trees proved to be ineffective, so Hopkins advocated destroying the beetles by cutting infested trees and shipping the logs to mills at non-forested locations or peeling bark from infested trees while in the woods. However, until 1906, sale of green trees was prohibited, including infested trees that were not yet faded. Thus, control action rested solely on peeling infested bark.

Other people also had ideas about controlling the beetle. Mr. Tinsley of Custer, SD, developed a cutting tool with removable handles for stripping bark up to a height of 25 ft on standing trees. In addition, Mr. Yarbray, also of Custer, wanted "$50 cash, a lineman's outfit, 20 miles of insulated No. 12 copper wire, a safety belt, and a saddle horse." With them, he promised to rid the Hills of the beetle. Hopkins noted: "It would appear that he contemplates electrocuting the beetles individually or collectively…. It is too bad we have to turn down such advanced ideas." Still others went about transplanting "slime" that they believed was killing beetles.

Whatever perils brought about the beetles' demise, the outbreak, which had killed one billion bd ft of pine, waned after 1906 and Hopkins set about finding evidence that his recommendations were responsible. His final word on the matter was to Forest Assistant John Murdock, 20 December 1910: "There is no trace of doubt in my mind that if my recommendation in 1901 and 1902 had been promptly adopted and carried out, there would have been no further loss of timber from the work of the beetles…. The Forest Service should certainly profit by this expensive experience." (Furniss 1997).

Colorado Next in Line

On 12 August 1902, Hopkins received specimens of the Black Hills beetle from pine trees near Bailey, CO, submitted by State Entomologist C. P. Gillette. This was the first authentic record of its existence in Colorado. During a special investigation in May, 1903, Hopkins found the same species in northwestern New Mexico in the vicinity of Vermejo, where it was killing the mature pine trees over a large area (Hopkins 1906).

On 14 July 1905, Gillette wrote that a large amount of timber was dying in the vicinity of Palmer Lake, CO. The specimens sent with his letter proved to be the Black Hills beetle. In the meantime, people interested in the protection of the forests in the vicinity of Colorado Springs had inaugurated a campaign to control the beetle. Professor Lawrence Bruner of the University of Nebraska was hired to provide technical assistance.

Under Professor Bruner's direction, 600 to 800 trees on private lands near Glen Eyrie and Colorado Springs were felled during August to October, and the bark removed and burned to kill the infesting insects.

Hopkins consulted with Pinchot, then investigated the situation around the Pikes Peak Reserve 5 to 13 October 1905. With characteristic detail, he described his survey by foot trails, train, wagon, and saddle (Hopkins 1905):

> "Beginning on the morning of October 5 explorations were made as follows: Glen Eyrie trail on mountain northward, returning via Douglass Canyon; October 6, from Glen Eyrie by way of Colorado City, Bear Creek Canyon, High Line road, to Bruin Inn, returning by way of North Cheyenne Canyon, Colorado Springs, and Palmer Park; October 7, from Glen Eyrie by way of Manitou, over Crystal Park trail to Crystal Park, returning by the Bear Creek trail, Bear Creek Canyon, and Colorado Springs; October 8, from Glen Eyrie, by way of Blair Athol, Pike View, Pope Ranch, and Palmer Park; October 9, from Colorado Springs by way of Colorado Springs and Cripple Creek Railway to Clyde, thence by wagon to an altitude of about 10,000 feet, returning by same route to Colorado Springs; October 10, from Colorado Springs by way of the Colorado Midland Railroad to Woodland Park, thence by wagon to Manitou Park; October 11, by saddle from Manitou Park east to Palmer Lake, thence by wagon southeast by way of Rusted to Woodland Ranch; October 12, in the Colorado pinery on the Arkansas and Platte divide; October 13, in the Colorado pinery, returning by way of Colorado Springs to Glen Eyrie."

Additional explorations were made on the 12th and 13th by W. D. Edmonston, under Hopkins' instructions, in the vicinity of Palmer Lake. Edmonston was Head Ranger of the Pikes Peak Forest Reserve. He was designated by Forest Supervisor Clarke as the proper official to receive instructions in the identification of the infested trees to be felled and barked to kill the principal insect enemies. Edmonston was destined to play a prominent role in forest entomology as an employee of the USDA Bureau of Entomology, Division of Forest Insect Investigations, in Colorado and Arizona.

William Douglas Edmonston

William Douglas Edmonston (1870-1936) (fig. 3) was born in Edinburgh, Scotland. A graduate of the School of Fine Arts of the University of Edinburgh, he was an artist of considerable ability and exhibited some of his water colors at the Royal Scottish Academy and at the Royal Academy of England. He came to the United States in 1890 and settled at Brunston near Larkspur, CO.

USDA Forest Service Gen. Tech. Rep. RMRS-GTR-195. 2007

3

Figure 3. William D. Edmonston at Colorado Springs, 1927 (Burke 1946).

ing specimens and taking biological notes for Hopkins' taxonomic specialists in the various insect groups (for example, bark beetles, wood borers, parasitic wasps).

In 1924, Edmonston and Hofer were involved with a Black Hills beetle control project on the Kaibab. Evidently, things didn't go well. As F. P. Keen of the Berkeley Forest Insect Laboratory (FIL) recounted (Maunder 1977):

"I was assigned to the Kaibab control project in 1924 (fig. 4) because the Forest Service was not satisfied with the work that Edmonston and Hofer were doing down there, so I was sent down to direct and supervise this project. I found out that (they) had no systematic method of spotting the bug infested trees, so I set up a systematic spotting of the area... we soon found a number of infested trees in gulches that they had missed. Since the infested trees were concentrated in large groups (fig. 5), I recommended that instead of peeling the bark on individual trees ... they cut and pile the infested trees ... and then burn the whole pile.

In 1901, Edmonston became a ranger on what is now the Pike National Forest. From 5 to 13 October 1905, he made several trips in the vicinity of Colorado Springs and Palmer Lake with Hopkins to study infestations of the Black Hills beetle. From then on, Edmonston spent considerable time cruising bark beetle infestations and conducting control operations in the various forests of Colorado. Sometime in 1907 or 1908, he was assigned to the Bureau of Entomology from the Forest Service to work under the direction of Hopkins on the practical application of insect control in the national forests of Colorado, southern Wyoming, and eastern Utah. Edmonston experimented with methods of treating trees infested with the Black Hills beetle, including felling the infested trees, sawing them into lumber, and burning the slabs.

In October 1913, he established the Southern Rocky Mountain station at Colorado Springs assisted by Agent George Hofer. From 1913 to 1924, Colorado Springs was the headquarters of the Southern Rocky Mountain station, but considerable time was spent at Sabino Canyon near Tucson. The work in Arizona consisted of collect-

Figure 4. From left: F. C. Craighead, W. D. Edmonston, G. Hofer, and F. P. Keen at Mile-and-a-Half Cabin, Kaibab National Forest, AZ, 3 September 1924. Craighead was second Chief of Forest Insect Investigations, Washington, D.C.; Edmonston and Hofer were stationed in the Rocky Mountains. Keen was on a detail from the Palo Alto, CA, station to supervise control of a bark beetle outbreak (Berkeley Forest Insect Laboratory photo 5548).

4

USDA Forest Service Gen. Tech. Rep. RMRS-GTR-195. 2007

Figure 5. In 1924, Paul Keen was dispatched to the Kaibab National Forest, AZ, from the Berkeley Forest Insect Laboratory to supervise control of a Black Hills beetle outbreak in which large groups of ponderosa pine were being killed such as is shown here. The trees were felled, piled, and burned—a practice that sometimes ignited unwanted fires (Photo FC- 253 by F.P. Keen).

At first the Forest Service didn't approve of the use of fire in this manner because they were afraid that the fires would get away. I finally convinced the Service that if we burned the piles while there was snow on the ground there would be little hazard of the fire escaping. So the Supervisor approved. The crews proceeded to pile the trees … but didn't start burning until we had a general snow. Then they … burned all the piles at once. Most of the piles burned up satisfactorily, but fire from about six of the piles jumped the line and caused some problems. Then the Forest Service people said, 'Oh, it was a disaster.' They claimed that they could see the smoke and flames clear across the canyon and that the flames were three hundred feet in the air. They said there were three or four hundred acres involved. I doubted that, so I went out and mapped in the burned area, and found that one area was thirty acres and another was forty acres … . I also found that there was very little damage to any of the residual trees.

That was the second year I was there. It was the last year we had funds to do anything, but we had cleaned up most of the main area of infestation north of Jacob Lake. We had one really bad spot where … practically every tree was infested, a tremendous big group. We finally decided that we were not going to be able to treat all the big groups like this, and we adopted the strategy of working on the perimeter somewhat like fighting a big forest fire. This method seemed to work and I got credit for having stopped the infestation."

In 1925 and 1926, Edmonston and Hofer assisted M. W. Blackman in his experimental work on the Black Hills beetle on the Kaibab. The results of this work were published by Blackman in Technical Publication 36 of the New York State College of Forestry titled "The Black Hills Beetle."

In February, 1928, Edmonston was transferred to the Pacific Slope Forest Insect Laboratory at Palo Alto, CA, where he remained until his retirement for disability on

USDA Forest Service Gen. Tech. Rep. RMRS-GTR-195. 2007

5

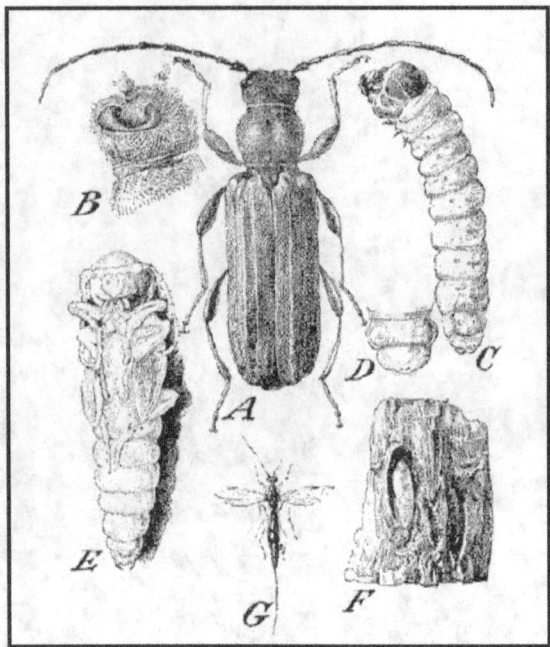

Figure 6. A longhorn beetle, *Tetropium abietis* Fall (Coleopters: Cerambycidae), drawn by W. D. Edmonston. It appeared as Fig. 66 in Keen (1939).

1 August 1932. Edmonston spent most of the time at the Palo Alto lab working on insect life history charts and drawings of forest and shade tree insects (fig. 6). Many of these were used in several bulletins of the Department and in other publications. He died in Tucson 7 November 1936.

George Hofer

George Hofer (1863-1944) (fig. 7) was selected for permanent appointment as Agent by Edmonston from among the woodsmen employed on the Northeastern Oregon western pine beetle control project (Burke and Wickman 1990). He was born in Switzerland. Previous to his employment by the Bureau of Entomology, he was engaged in mining activities around Sumpter, OR.

Edmonston had Hofer with him on all of his moves after the Northeastern Oregon project terminated in 1911. They were together at field stations at Klamath Falls and Ashland, OR, Colorado Springs, and Tucson. Hofer was promoted from Agent to Entomological Ranger and then to Scientific Aid. He had reached the Senior Grade when he was retired for disability in October, 1927.

Hofer was a careful worker and much of his time was spent collecting and studying the biology of forest insects in Colorado and Arizona. Many of the records on round-headed borers published by F. C. Craighead, and on flatheaded borers published by H. E. Burke, were made by Hofer. He published Farmers Bulletin 1154, "The Aspen Borer and How to Control It," and with Craighead, Bulletin 1197, "Protection of Mesquite Cordwood and Posts from Borers." Hofer died at his home near Sabino Canyon, AZ, on 25 March 1944, at age 80.

Fort Collins 1935 to 1940

A Forest Insect Laboratory (FIL) was established in Denver in 1935 with James A. Beal (1898-1985) in charge. Noel D. Wygant (1908-1992) joined the staff that year. The following account is from the oral history interview of Wygant by Larson (1979a) with minimal alteration of the transcript. In the summer of 1935, the USDA Forest Service established the Rocky Mountain Forest and Range Experiment Station on the campus of Colorado A & M College at Fort Collins. Dr. Richard McArdle was director. He, along with Dr. Morrel, Dean of the Forestry College, invited the members of the FIL to move to the campus. The laboratory was moved there in late summer of 1935. Personnel of this period are shown in figures 8 and 9.

Wygant's assignment was to work on the insects affecting shelterbelts. This was a major project developed by a number of foresters interested in trying to improve the climate of the Great Plains and stop some of the wind and dust. He

Figure 7. George Hofer (Burke 1946).

Figure 8. Western personnel of Division of Forest Insect Investigations at Pingree Park, CO, ca 1937 to 38. Front row from left: F. C. Craighead, Chief, Washington, D.C.; D. De Leon; J. A. Beal; C. L. Massey; J. C. Evenden; unknown; and W. Howe. Back row: G. R. Hopping; unknown; F. P. Keen; J. M. Miller; and N. D. Wygant. Photo provided by J. M. Schmid.

Figure 9. Personnel of Fort Collins, CO, Forest Insect Laboratory, 1939. Front row from left: James A. Beal, in charge (later Chief of Forest Insect Investigations, Washington, D.C.); Rachel Overing, Sec.; and Donald De Leon. Back: Dwight Hester; Calvin L. Massey; Wayne Howe; and Noel D. Wygant (later head of the laboratory). Photo provided by J. M. Schmid.

worked in Nebraska, South Dakota (fig. 10), Oklahoma, and Kansas. Prior to 1935, Lynn Baumhaufer, a forest entomologist working out of the Coeur d'Alene, ID, FIL, spent several summers at Halsey on the Nebraska NF studying pine tip moths that were severely damaging the pine plantations. The main problem insects were borers in cottonwood and ash and foliage-feeders, such as grasshoppers and other miscellaneous insects. The trees were growing under a great deal of stress and as a result, many of the so-called secondary insects, or less aggressive insects, killed many of the trees.

During 1935 to 1939, Beal, Baumhaufer, Dwight Hester, and John W. "Jack" Whiteside were located in Fort Collins. Except for Baumhaufer and Beal, who gave part of their time to problems in the Great Plains, much of the work was directed toward studies of the Black Hills beetle and to technical assistance to the Forest Service and other forest landowners experiencing insect problems. At that time, the principal problem

USDA Forest Service Gen. Tech. Rep. RMRS-GTR-195. 2007

7

Figure 10. Sampling white grubs in soil at a forest tree nursery, Baltic, SD, August 7, 1936. Photo FC-227 by N. D. Wygant.

was the Black Hills beetle. A few defoliators, such as a pandora moth and the Great Basin tent caterpillar, were also of concern.

Robert L. Furniss (1908 - 1980) moved to Fort Collins from the Portland, OR, FIL in spring of 1940, replacing Beal who left to teach at Duke University. The Fort Collins staff also included Don De Leon, who replaced Baumhaufer who transferred to Beltsville, MD, in 1938. However, the Fort Collins Lab was closed only 3 months after Furniss arrived. In those few months, Bob set about getting acquainted with his new territory, including climbing Rocky Mountain peaks (fig. 11) as he had done in the Cascades of Oregon and Washington as a Mazama. He also made a field trip to the Dixie NF, UT, to examine a mealybug on Engelmann spruce.

The closure of the Fort Collins lab resulted from an affront to a Congressman from Vermont. The Bureau of Entomology and Plant Quarantine (BE&PQ), of which the Division of Forest Insect Investigations (FII) was a part, administered the USDA insect control programs, including Dutch elm disease and the gypsy moth in the northeast. At that time, they were trying to control the disease, and as soon as a diseased tree was found, it had to be removed under federal and state laws. The Congressman had some elm trees removed from his property that were diseased and he didn't want them removed. He became very upset that the federal bureaucrats had removed these trees and saw to it that

Dutch elm disease would receive a drastic cut in appropriations. Unfortunately, he directed his energy in the wrong direction. He thought he was trying to curtail the funds for Dutch elm disease control when in reality it was forest insect research.

Lee Strong, Chief of BE&PQ, told Dr. F. C. Craighead, Chief of FII, that he had to come up with cuts and where he would apply the cuts. Craighead applied the cuts percentage-wise across all the laboratories, but the pressure from the west coast industries was so great against cutting the California and Portland labs that Strong was told that he couldn't cut those so heavily. At that time, Paul Keen at Portland, and John Miller at the Berkeley, CA. FIL, had some major projects underway on the susceptibility of ponderosa pine to attack by the western pine beetle. Their programs had a lot of industry and forester support. Craighead, in turn, was given an edict to cut out one station. They decided that it would be the Fort Collins FIL, and it was closed 1 July 1940. De Leon and Wygant were transferred to Berkeley. Bob Furniss returned to Portland.

Figure 11. Robert L. Furniss at Estes Park, CO, after his transfer to Fort Collins from Portland, OR, in 1940. Photo by Frances Furniss.

In 1940 and 1941, insect problems were developing in Forest Service Regions 2 and 3 (including Colorado and New Mexico). Wygant was sent to New Mexico to assess the Great Basin tent caterpillar problem in the aspen stands. Thousands of acres were being defoliated and fishermen, picnickers, and others were complaining because of the vast number of caterpillars.

Fort Collins Lab Reopened — 1942

These insect problems resulted in reopening the Fort Collins lab on 1 July 1942, with Wygant in charge. Many of the younger forest entomologists were in military service so staffing was inadequate. Wygant recalled: " I was supposed to attend to all the insect problems in New Mexico, Arizona, Utah, Colorado, Wyoming, and South Dakota plus the Great Plains. Most of my time was spent in examining and evaluating the various infestations present at that time."

Spruce Beetle

In the summer of 1943, a District Ranger on the White River NF reported a bark beetle infestation in Englemann spruce on the White River Plateau north of Glenwood Springs, CO. In September, he and Wygant took a 5-day trip on horseback and discovered that the infestation extended over 500,000 acres. The bark beetle was identified as the Englemann spruce beetle (now called the "spruce beetle," *Dendroctonus rufipennis*). Calvin L. Massey (1914-1984), who had studied entomology at Duke University under Beal, was employed to study the biology of the beetle on the White River NF. Massey discovered that the beetle had a 2-year cycle instead of 1-year as reported by A. D. Hopkins. Also, George R. Struble from the Berkeley FIL was assigned to study the biology of the beetle on the Grand Mesa NF, CO, where another outbreak was located. He discovered that most of the beetles overwinter in their second year as adults beneath the bark at the base of the trees. This habit has an important bearing on the ability of this beetle to survive the cold winters of the sub-alpine zone. A comprehensive account of this outbreak is contained in Massey and Wygant (1954).

Trap Trees

In retrospect, it was determined that the outbreak on the White River NF and elsewhere developed in trees blown down by a severe windstorm on 30 June 1939.

Subsequent studies disclosed that, if there were felled logs or windthrown trees available, the beetles preferred these trees to standing trees. Thus, interest focused on use of trap trees. A trap tree is a green spruce tree that is felled just prior to the flight of the beetle. David McComb, a summer employee working on his Masters degree, and Roy Nagel, who was transferred from Beltsville, MD, found that the number of attacks per square foot in windthrown or felled trees was approximately 10 times that on standing trees. Hence, it looked as though one trap tree would absorb the population from up to 10 standing trees.

The beetle flies in June and early July, so trap trees must be felled in the previous fall or early spring. They were located along roads where they could be hauled to a mill where the infested slabs could be burned. Problems resulted in some cases where trap trees were felled ahead of the building of roads. By the time the roads were built and the timber sale awarded, the beetles had already flown from the trap trees. As a result, the trap tree method lost its appeal.

Chemical Treatment

Most infested trees were sprayed with orthodichlorobenzene in fuel oil using a method developed at the Coeur d'Alene FIL for control of the mountain pine beetle. It was used during the 1949 and 1950 control campaigns to spray trunks of standing trees to a height of about 35 feet. Bob Chism from the BE&PQ, Morristown, NJ, was assigned to the laboratory and, with Massey, developed a water emulsion spray. Because water was available in the forest, this spray eliminated the need to transport large quantities of fuel oil to inaccessible locations (fig. 12). In 1950 and 1951, an emulsion of ethylene dibromide proved to be effective and cheaper than orthodichlorobenzene and was used against both the spruce beetle and Black Hills beetle (fig. 13).

Tom T. Terrell transferred from the Coeur d'Alene FIL to Fort Collins in 1944 to help with the spruce beetle survey. Tom had a lot of experience with surveys of the mountain pine beetle in Idaho and Montana and was the ideal person to spearhead the surveys of the spruce beetle. His work involved sampling infested trees on the ground and conducting aerial surveys. Later, Amel Landgraf, Fred B. Knight (see Appendix A), and seasonal employees helped on the aerial surveys. Aerial surveys are not useful for early detection of spruce beetle outbreaks because the trees infested by the beetle in July and August do not fade until the following spring. Even then

USDA Forest Service Gen. Tech. Rep. RMRS-GTR-195. 2007

9

Figure 12. Packing orthodichlorobenzene insecticide for spraying Engelmann spruce infested with the spruce beetle, Arapaho National Forest, CO, August 1950 (Photo WO-462737A by L. J. Prater).

Some believed that much of the Englemann spruce type in Colorado—which was over-mature and highly susceptible—could be lost unless control measures were taken. After review of the surveys and research results, a control project was proposed for the season of 1950. There was very much debate. Robert Furniss, Paul Keen, and John Miller were opposed to this method based on their experience with outbreaks of the western pine beetle and the mountain pine beetle in California and Oregon. The outcome didn't warrant the expenditure, so their philosophy carried through to the proposed spruce beetle control. On the other extreme were some naturalists who said control must be achieved at any cost. The issue attracted two congressional investigations. Some congressmen flew over the area to view the dead spruce, and two members of the Congressional Finance Committee reviewed the proposal. The project would cost about 2 million dollars—a lot of money in 1949. Finally, it was decided that a project would be undertaken in 1950.

In 1950, 1 million trees were treated with ortho-dichlorobenzene or ethylene dibromide. Several large camps were setup by the Forest Service on the White River, Routt, Holy Cross, and Arapaho NFs (fig. 14) for the spring project. The program was carried out

the needles tend to drop off before they become the characteristically yellowish color that pine trees display after being infested with bark beetles. So, surveys were mostly done on the ground.

From 1944 to 1951, Terrell and his crews were responsible for both the detection of new outbreaks and measuring the mortality of spruce in the old outbreaks. By 1949, the mortality from the beetle had reached more than 3 billion board feet on the White River NF (Wygant and Nelson 1949). By that time, most of the larger trees were killed, so efforts now focused on possibly preventing the flight of the beetles out of that area into adjacent national forests. Surveys of the spruce beetle were made in the surrounding forests to determine where the beetles might have flown. The airport at Eagle, CO, was closed for 2 days in June because the beetles were so abundant. On the White River Plateau, drowned beetles were reported to be a foot deep and 8 to 10 feet wide for a distance of a mile on the leeward side of Trappers Lake.

Figure 13. Mel McKnight spraying ethylene di-bromide insecticide on a ponderosa pine infested with the Black Hills beetle, Lookout Mountain, Golden, CO, June 1959 (Fort Collins Forest Insect Laboratory photo FC-823 by A. E. Langraf).

Figure 14. Spruce forest in Piney Ridge Basin, Arapaho NF, CO, where 50,000 trees, infested by the spruce beetle, were sprayed with insecticide in 1950 (Photo WO-462780 by L. J. Prater).

efficiently; however, surveys that fall indicated that the outbreak was by no means under control and an equally large or larger project would be necessary in 1951.

That project never came about due to the intervention of nature. On 1 February 1951, an all-time low temperature was recorded by mountain weather stations in Colorado. For example, the low temperature at Eagle was –59° F. It was known from laboratory tests that larvae were killed at –32° F and adults died at –12° F. Survey crews were sent out on snowcats, snowshoes, and skis to collect samples. These samples indicated that 90 percent of the beetle population was killed by the freeze. Fewer beetles enhanced the effect of woodpeckers, which had increased to a very high level, and they further reduced the number of beetles that were able to infest trees in the summer of 1951.

Freeze Got the Black Hills Beetle, too—for a While

The freeze was widespread throughout the Rocky Mountains. It also had a pronounced effect on the Black Hills beetle, now known as the mountain pine beetle (MPB), in the Black Hills of South Dakota and on the Front Range of Colorado. Surveys showed that approximately 90 percent of the population was killed. The concern and need for direct control measures was alleviated for several years until the population had a chance to build up again. By the mid-1950s, beetles had

built up to epidemic proportion, both in the Black Hills and on the Front Range.

As mentioned, Robert Furniss and Paul Keen favored selective cutting of high risk or susceptible ponderosa pine for management of the western pine beetle. However, Keen spent a week with Wilford and Wygant looking at infested young stands of ponderosa pine in the northern Black Hills. The trees were mostly 60 to 80 years old and in overstocked stands. There appeared to be no selectivity on the part of the beetles for any specific class of tree. Keen agreed that what worked against the western pine beetle wouldn't necessarily be effective against the MPB in these stands. In subsequent years, J. M. Schmid showed that partial cutting to reduce stand density reduced pine mortality caused by the MPB (see Appendix B).

For lack of a better method, attention turned to testing lindane, a contact insecticide. Massey found that Black Hills beetles were killed when allowed to crawl over filter papers coated with equivalent of one-twentieth of a pound of lindane per acre. A pilot test involving 100 acres was set up in the Black Hills in cooperation with the Beltsville, MD, laboratory. Up to 2 pounds of lindane were applied per acre repeatedly for a period of 2 or 3 days, "The foliage and bark of the trees literally glistened with the insecticide." Inexplicably, there were more infested trees in the treated area than in untreated areas. A similar case was encountered with DDT against the pine tip moth in the Nebraska NF. The DDT was applied the first year at rates of 1 and 2 pounds per acre. Excellent results were obtained that year, but repeated tests produced no treatment effect.

Spruce Budworm

During the latter part of the spruce beetle episode, outbreaks of the western spruce budworm were beginning in southern Colorado, in particular, and in Rocky Mountain National Park. DDT was just becoming available and the Forest Service requested that some experimental test-spraying be done. Leslie W. Orr, from the Beltsville laboratory, was assigned to do this study. DDT was applied with excellent results from the ground in Rocky Mountain NP using a high pressure sprayer. However, aerial spraying of 30 acres near Estes Park in the following year produced inconclusive results. The spray was applied in mid-June, but was followed by a freeze that killed the new growth on the Douglas-fir. As a result, many of the caterpillars starved to death on the sprayed plots as well as on the unsprayed plots. So, the effectiveness of spraying couldn't be measured.

Noel Wygant recalled the following story: "When you do aerial spraying, you get up about four o'clock in the morning and be out there with your plane loaded to take off at daybreak. ... a Denver Post reporter was planning to make an account of it and he said, 'Well, boys, I don't get up at four o'clock so I'll see you later in the day.' He wrote his story the night before and sent it in. It turned out the next morning that the wind was too high so we didn't spray. We weren't able to spray for 3 more days. Coincidentally, the cedar wax wing migration was taking place in the city of Loveland. At the same time, a severe ice and snow storm occurred there, killing many of these birds. An article came out in the Denver Post about the effects of DDT spraying on the bird life, although Loveland was 30 miles away from where we had applied the DDT."

Fort Collins, Post 1968

Wygant retired in 1968 (he died in Fort Collins on 1 May 1992 at age 84) and was replaced as Project Leader by Robert E. Stevens, who transferred from the Washington Office. Stevens cooperated with Frank Hawksworth, a mistletoe taxonomist at RM, on studies of insects infesting dwarf mistletoes (Stevens and Hawksworth 1984), and with PNW entomologists on defoliating moths and MPB-ponderosa pine interactions (Sartwell and Stevens

1975). John M. Schmid joined the staff in 1966 after three seasons of summer work (see Appendix B). During the period 1959 to 1973, Melvin E. McKnight also worked for RM, stationed initially at Fort Collins and later as Project Leader at Bottineau, ND (see Appendix C). William F. McCambridge (1923-2007) worked at Fort Collins during two periods: 1948 to 1952 and 1962 to 1981. Among his accomplishments was the development of a spray to prevent infestation of ponderosa pine by the mountain pine beetle (fig. 15) (McCambridge 1982). Stephen A. Mata assisted McKnight, McCambridge, and Schmid in their studies throughout his exceptional career as a technician beginning in 1964 (see Appendix D). Personnel of the Fort Collins forest insect research project in 1973 are shown in figure 16.

Figure 15. An emulsified spray was developed by Bill McCambridge to protect individual ponderosa pine from attack by the mountain pine beetle in recreational areas of the Black Hills, SD, and Colorado (McCambridge 1982). Photo provided by S. A. Mata.

USDA Forest Service Gen. Tech. Rep. RMRS-GTR-195. 2007

Figure 16. Personnel of Forest Insect Research at Fort Collins, CO, 1973. Front, left to right: Gladys Turner and Esther Hanson (clerical staff); Standing: John Schmid (Entomologist), Jim Mitchell (Technician), Steve Mata (Technician), Robert E. Stevens (Project Leader), and William F. McCambridge (Entomologist). Photo provided by R. E. Stevens.

Albuquerque Laboratory Established in 1952

Jack W. Bongberg (1911-1976) was transferred from the Berkeley FIL to Albuquerque, NM, to establish a forest insect and disease laboratory effective 1 September 1952. The area served was Arizona and New Mexico. He transferred to Washington, D.C. in 1955. Calvin L. Massey (1914-1984) replaced Bongberg and remained in Albuquerque until his retirement in 1972. William F. McCambridge worked in Albuquerque from 1958 to 1960, assigned to study the piñon needle scale, *Matsucoccus acalypyus* Herbert, in Mesa Verde and Grand Canyon National Parks (McCambridge 1974). McCambridge had transferred to Albuquerque after being the first forest entomologist assigned to Alaska (1952 to 1957). R. K. Bennett was in Albuquerque with Bongberg, and M. J. Stelzer and J. F. Chansler were there with Massey in 1962 on a project titled: "Biology, Ecology, and Control of Bark Beetles and Defoliators in the Southwest" (Price 1976). Dan Jennings was in Albuquerque intermittently and in various capacities from 1960 until the lab closed in 1976 (See Appendix E). He then transferred to Maine to work on the eastern spruce budworm.

Calvin L. Massey

Cal Massey was born in Denver, 20 November 1914 (Larson 1979b). His interest in entomology came about indirectly. He suffered a broken neck in high school football and because of it, he received a scholarship to Colorado A&M College from the State Rehabilitation Service. There, he took instruction from several inspirational teachers ("Miss Palmer," an aphid specialist; "Dr. List, who was an excellent entomologist"; and "John Hoerner, who was probably more interested in students than any man that I have known."). While he was a student at Colorado A & M, worked during one summer for the Fort Collins lab in the Black Hills on a study of Black Hills beetle seasonal history. During another summer, he assisted with studies of the pandora moth on the Arapaho NF and the cottonwood borer on the Shelter Belt Project. In 1939, he enrolled at Duke University and received a MA (pandora moth life history) and a Ph.D. (1943) on bark beetles of North Carolina. In 1944, he was employed by Noel Wygant at the Fort Collins lab to study the Engelmann spruce beetle.

Massey became interested in nematodes that he found infesting the spruce beetle (Massey 1956). He contacted Gerald Thorne, a retired nematologist, formerly with Agricultural Research Service, then living in Salt Lake City. Through Thorne's tutelage, Massey went on to describe many bark beetle nematodes. I am aware that some conflict developed regarding the Thorne-Massey concepts and those of their counter-parts at the University of California, Berkeley. But that seems universal in matters as subjective as the classification of organisms.

I became interested in parasitic nematodes in 1956 while studying the Douglas-fir beetle, *Dendroctonus pseudotsuge* Hopkins, at Boise (INT). This led to communicating with Massey to learn his procedure for mounting and preserving such nematodes on glass slides for identification. With his help, five species of nematodes were identified from this beetle (Furniss 1967).

In 1961, I went to Albuquerque to receive training in nematode identification. Prior to my arrival, Massey had not made any preparations, merely spread out some slides and reprints, and then left. While he was gone, I had difficulty focusing the microscope and sought to adjust it. Then, I looked at his type slides and drawings and could not see some illustrated features on the slides. So, when he returned, I made it known that I had adjusted the microscope, but he didn't like that I had

USDA Forest Service Gen. Tech. Rep. RMRS-GTR-195. 2007

13

tampered with it. He suggested that I wasn't able to see some of the features so clear in the drawings because I didn't have as much experience as he did. I was left to presume that his published drawings must represent a composite of slides, each of which showed better some features than others.

While I was there, I learned why a nematode from my Douglas-fir beetle study had been identified by Massey only to genus (*Parasitaphelenchus* sp.). He explained that only the larval (immature) stage occurs in the beetle's body cavity, whereas the mature stage, which occurs in the frass of the beetle's gallery, is needed for specific identification. So, when I returned home, I put frass in a Berlese funnel and got adults, which Massey later described as *P. beccus* Massey (Massey 1974) although he omitted the type locality (Moscow Mountain, Latah County, ID). His publication (Massey 1974) is a valuable resource, not likely to be supplanted in the foreseeable future.

Throughout the 30 years since Massey retired, the whereabouts of his nematode slide collection (including holotypes from which he described new species) was unknown. During preparation of this manuscript in April 2006, I made a last effort to locate them. Through extraordinary luck, I learned that the collection was discovered in 2001 in a closet in deteriorating condition and is now at the Harold W. Manter Laboratory of Parasitology, W 529 Nebraska Hall, University of Nebraska-Lincoln. The collection consists of 1,800 slides including 134 holotypes. It is unknown why slides of such immense scientific importance were not deposited in the U.S. National Collection or other suitable repository.

Northern Rocky Mountains

Josef Brunner

Josef Brunner (fig. 17) came to Montana from Bavaria in 1898 to hunt big game and write outdoor articles. His book, "Tracks and Tracking," was published for the Boy Scouts (Brunner 1909). While hunting in the Little Snowy Mountains, he noticed extensive killing of lodgepole pine, *Pinus contorta* Douglas, by bark beetles and wrote (2 January 1909) to Chief Forester Gifford Pinchot in Washington, D.C., wanting to know "… the name of the little bug which makes the inner bark of freshly fallen trees (pine, spruce, fir) its primary breeding place and then attacks en masse nearby standing

green trees? … the name is wanted for use in a magazine article into which I do not wish any mistake to find its way." The letter was forwarded to Hopkins. The two men corresponded further and Brunner's interest in forest insects led Hopkins to hire him on 1 July 1909 as Agent and Expert at $1,200 per annum (Furniss 2003).

An experience that shaped Brunner's studies and related them to fire was detailed in his letter to Hopkins, 8 October 1913: "I returned yesterday from the trip up the Clearwater River. I was only two days off hunting as I found so much of interest in the forest insect line up there that hunting became a matter of less consequence to me." Near Rainy Lake, he found thousands of lodgepole pine trees infested with larvae of a pitch moth, *Vespamima sequoiae*. Their feeding injury to the inner bark caused up to 5 pounds of pitch to be exuded from a single tree. Brunner believed that the highly flammable pitch intensified forest fires. This belief, and his subsequent studies of pitch moths (Brunner 1914, 1915), fueled his ongoing conflict with the Forest Service regarding the relationships and importance of insects versus wildfires. On 29 January 1916, he wrote to Hopkins: "I am getting toward the end with the paper on Fire and Insects …" Hopkins mentioned that the paper would have to be reviewed by the Forest Service. Brunner got excited (17 October 1916) at the mention of the Forest Service and wanted assurance that he would see their criticism. If too critical, he vowed to add some scandalous stuff about a tie sale in the Clinton area that was struck from the original manuscript. "This is the clearest case of 'Raubwirthshaft' (plundering) and

Figure 17. Josef Brunner (left) and Jack L. Webb on a field trip in Montana during July, 1910 (Burke 1946).

worse than any practiced by the so-called 'timer (timber) wolves,' which came under my observation. If they do not like it now the only way to bring them to reason is to bring out the truth unvarnished and let them answer publicly for their plunders." The paper was never published, however, due to a growing rift between him and Hopkins that resulted in Brunner leaving the Service in June 1917 (Furniss 2003).

Postscript: In 1950, when I was hired, older personnel of the Division of Forest Insect Investigations, Bureau of Entomology and Plant Quarantine, still sought to show that insects caused greater loss of trees than did forest fires. In an ironic twist of fate, FII was abolished in 1953 and its personnel, including me, were transferred to the Forest Service. However, by then forest entomology was taking new directions and the issue died on its own.

James C. Evenden

On 30 June 1914, Brunner wrote to Hopkins that James C. Evenden (fig. 18) was on the Civil Service list of persons who passed the test for the Entomological Ranger position. Brunner commented (6 July 1914): "If Evenden… takes the place of Fleming (who resigned) I hope he is city broke and does not make a fool of himself when he gets into town after being out in camp, like they all seem to do" (Furniss 2003).

Evenden was appointed Entomological Ranger at $900 per annum on 1 October or as soon as he could terminate his employment with the Forest Service on the Mount Hood District, OR, and report to Brunner. Again, Brunner casts his doubts (3 August 1914): "After Oct. 1th, Mr. Evenden, if not hardened in to outdoor life, will find camping rather disagreeable and I should not be surprised, if he did not leave us in the lurch again when the rigor of our winters become full blown. I hope he will pan out o.k. but I expect to hear a lot of kicking never the less on account of unpleasant weather conditions, if he is a greenhorn in the woods. Well, we will see" (Furniss 2003).

Evenden arrived in Missoula, MT, on 6 October 1914 and got instructions from Brunner to proceed to Potomac, MT, near what was to be Evenden's winter camp. Arriving at the so-called winter camp 2 days later, Evenden was dismayed to find: "… that the camp consisted of a 7 x 9-ft tent, some bedding rolled up in one corner, a fire ring of stones out in front with a frying pan and a few other cooking utensils, but no food to cook" (Larson 1979c). He retreated to the community of Potomac, MT, for the night and on the next day "rustled some old lumber, an

old cooking stove with no legs, and a heating stove and returned to camp." Most of the items were given to him by townspeople. He thought he would have returned home if train fare was available, however, in a few days he and Entomological Ranger Albert Wagner had set up a rather comfortable camp with separate tents for cooking and sleeping. On 24 October 1914, Brunner wrote Hopkins: "Have just returned from a trip to Wagner's and Evenden's camp … Evenden appears to be promising material and my fear that he might be rather a drag than a help in camp, I am glad to state, is entirely demolished" (Furniss 2003).

Evenden enlisted in the Army in May 1917 and served in Europe as a First Lieutenant and Captain in the 363rd Infantry, 91st Division, from August 1917 to June 1919. He was re-instated 15 June 1919 at Coeur d'Alene (fig. 19), and remained there throughout his career, retiring 31 December 1954.

Figure 18. James C. Evenden at a mountain pine beetle control camp, Big Hole Basin, MT, 1927 (Coeur d'Alene Forest Insect Laboratory Photo 352).

USDA Forest Service Gen. Tech. Rep. RMRS-GTR-195. 2007

15

Figure 19. Evenden in front of building in which the Coeur d'Alene, ID, Forest Insect Field Station was located from 1919 to 1923 (Coeur d'Alene Forest Insect Laboratory Photo 92).

Coeur d'Alene Forest Insect Laboratory 1919 to 1954

Henry J. Rust

Henry J. Rust (1878-1948) was the first person hired by Evenden (in 1921). Henry (fig. 20) was a keen observer, patient with detail, and a skilled photographer. He personally reared all insect material collected by him

Figure 20. Henry J. Rust. Photo provided by Barry Rust.

and others at the lab and kept detailed records, catalogs, and reports of the results, which were studies in themselves. Although he was not college-trained, he was assigned because of his abilities to study the biology of the pine engraver beetle and the role of predators in controlling the mountain pine beetle. He was deeply interested in mammals and birds and included their influence as predators in the latter study. He published on the mammals of Idaho (Rust 1946) and on his extraordinary study of the Pacific nighthawk on Tubbs Hill near Coeur d'Alene (Rust 1947).

Tom T. Terrell

Tom T. Terrell (1904-1985) was next to be hired. Terrell, a high school graduate, was launched unwittingly into a career in forest entomology in 1926 at age 22. He was reporting to work as a fire guard for the Forest Service in Montana when, "At Wisdom (Montana), I got on the wrong FS truck and ended up at a bark beetle control camp where I met Jim Evenden. Jim thought that I might be a good spotter (locating infested trees to be treated)."

In 1930, Terrell (fig. 21) made the first aerial survey of forest insect damage in the northern Rocky Mountains:

"The first flight of the survey could not be called auspicious; it was to be over Yellowstone National Park (YNP) from a field at Livingston, Montana. I had maps of the Park but nothing for the 65 miles between Livingston and the Park. The pilot had a railroad folder that showed a line going straight south to the Park. Away we went and got lost in the Absaroka Mountains where we were caught in a violent rainstorm. The plane was a small open-cockpit biplane, the pilot in the rear and me up front. The engine went quiet! Then loud pounding behind me! I was about to dive over the side and pull the ripcord when I discovered that the pilot was pounding on the plane to get my attention. He got it. He wanted to know if I didn't think we ought to go back? He had cut the engine so he could talk to me. I most certainly agreed with him. I was scared stiff. We made it back to the field where Jim Evenden was waiting. By that time the storm was real bad. The pilot taxied the plane up to the fence where we jumped out and with the help of Jim hung onto the plane and the fence to keep the plane on the ground until the storm let up. The pilot was Nick Mammer who later became a famous aviator in the region and one of the first mail and airline pilots in our area" (Terrell 1977).

Throughout the years, Terrell was involved in numerous other surveys, both on the ground and in the air, and in various control projects in YNP and adjacent national forests.

16

USDA Forest Service Gen. Tech. Rep. RMRS-GTR-195. 2007

Figure 21. Tom Terrell and the airplane he flew on the first aerial survey of forest insect damage in the northern Rocky Mountains in 1930 (Western Forest Insect Work Conference archives, unnumbered photo).

Reginald E. Balch

Reginald E. Balch (1894-1994) was another early employee at the Coeur d'Alene lab. He was born in England and immigrated to Canada at age 19. Following service during World War I and graduation from Syracuse University, he worked from 1928 to 1929 as a Forest Entomologist with the Coeur d'Alene lab. Thereafter he moved to Fredericton, New Brunswick, Canada, becoming Officer-in-Charge of the Forest Biology Laboratory where he attracted much acclaim for his work. Relevant here, he worked during 1929 in southwestern YNP at Bechler River Ranger Station studying competently, and in great detail, a budworm on lodgepole pine. He concluded (Balch 1930) that it must be a variety of the eastern spruce budworm, *Cacoecia fumiferana* var *lambertiana* Busck, but known now as a distinct species, the sugar pine tortrix, *Choristoneura lambertiana* (Busck), infesting pines in much of the west.

During that single season, he described the insect's life stages, life history and habits, natural control (parasites, predators); explored a method of representatively sampling the insect in trees; mapped the extent of the infestation; and determined the impact of defoliation on annual radial growth and mortality of infested trees. Although this insect was studied later (McGregor 1970), there is no reference in literature to Balch's outstanding and historically important study. Balch transferred to Fredericton, New Brunswick, Canada, soon afterward and other matters may have kept him from publishing this work.

Various other entomologists worked at the Coeur d'Alene lab during its existence (Larsen 1979c). Their work involved the biology and natural enemies (parasites and predators) of the mountain pine beetle (Donald De Leon); biology of the Douglas-fir beetle (William D. Bedard, Sr.); methods of controlling bark beetles (fig. 22), including toxic sprays (Archie L. Gibson); biology of the western spruce budworm; and surveys of insect infestations.

Figure 22. The mountain pine beetle was a major cause of white pine mortality in Idaho and various methods were developed in attempts to control it. One such method involved peeling bark while the broods were immature as shown here on the Coeur d'Alene National Forest ca 1930 (Coeur d'Alene Forest Insect Laboratory photo 488 by H. J. Rust).

USDA Forest Service Gen. Tech. Rep. RMRS-GTR-195. 2007

17

Throughout the existence of the Coeur d'Alene lab, results of all phases of work whether it be surveys, control supervision, or research were reported annually in typed reports. Usually nine copies were typed, consisting of the original and eight carbon copies. These reports were sent to whomever the subject of the report directly applied—Yellowstone NP, ranger districts, western labs such at Berkeley and Portland, Regional offices of the Forest Service, and the Washington Office. A total of 548 reports, mostly from the Coeur d'Alene and Missoula laboratories (during 1915 to 1958), were listed by Robert Denton (Denton 1959). Denton's mimeographed bibliography is deposited in the Special Collections Library, University of Idaho. Actual copies of the reports are scattered somewhat; most are presently in the Forest Service Region 1 office in the Federal Building, Missoula. Some of the reports pertaining to Yellowstone NP are in the archives at Mammoth Headquarters, WY.

Douglas-fir Tussock Moth

In May 1947, an armada of assorted aircraft took aloft in northern Idaho to control an outbreak of the Douglas-fir tussock moth that threatened to defoliate 400,000 acres of forest centered in Latah County. It was the largest aerial spraying project undertaken in western forests up to that time. Its successful outcome led to still larger projects involving another defoliator, the western spruce budworm, in vast areas of the northwestern US. This project also set a precedent for federal and state cost-sharing of forest insect control on private land (Furniss 2004).

Evenden was in charge of entomological aspects, assisted by Phillip C. Johnson who had transferred to Coeur d'Alene from the Berkeley FIL. No precedent existed for such large scale spraying of western forests. However, a spray consisting of 1 pound of DDT in 1 gallon of oil per acre had been used against the gypsy moth in the eastern US and was chosen for this project. Likewise, no contracts for such flying had been issued. Twenty-seven invitations to bid were sent to flying firms. Five responded.

Successful contractors were Johnson Flying Service, Missoula, MT, and Central Aircraft, Inc., Yakima, WA. Johnson's aircraft consisted of a Douglas DC-3 and two vintage Ford Tri-motors

(fig. 23 A). Central used a fleet of eight smaller, single-engine aircraft: Stearman biplanes, and Stinson, Fairchild, and Travelair monoplanes. The project was completed on 2 July. In the course of spraying, three of Central's aircraft crashed: a Travelair ground-looped while landing, another Travelair crashed because of engine failure, and a Stearman was caught in a downdraft at the head of a canyon (fig.23 B). The pilots were only slightly injured.

Looking back on the project, its importance went beyond its borders. Coincidentally, the western spruce budworm had begun to infest vast areas of forests in

Figure 23. A. Ford Tri-motor spraying DDT to control the Douglas-fir tussock moth in Latah County, ID, 1947. B. A crashed Stearman, one of three such accidents during this project. The project was the largest in the west at the time (Coeur d'Alene FIL photos by P. C. Johnson).

18

USDA Forest Service Gen. Tech. Rep. RMRS-GTR-195. 2007

Oregon and Washington. The apparent success of the Idaho tussock moth control project was monitored by counterparts in Oregon who tested the spray successfully against the budworm in 1948. Thereafter, 9 million acres were sprayed from 1949 to 1958, mostly in Oregon, Washington, and Idaho, but also Montana and the northern portion of Yellowstone National Park (Furniss and Renkin 2003). Spraying of the budworm included 1 million acres of the Boise NF and four surrounding national forests in 1955 — still the largest such project involving defoliators of Idaho forests. DDT was banned in the US in 1972, after which other insecticides were tested (including development of a formulation consisting of the tussock moth virus). However, spraying has generally diminished, in part because of a better understanding of the dynamics of these defoliators and forest composition, and development of preventive management practices.

Disbandment of Bureau of Entomology and Plant Quarantine — 1953

In 1953, President Eisenhower appointed ex-President Herbert Hoover to a head a commission to improve economy in government by reorganizing the Executive Departments. As a result, the Bureau of Entomology and Plant Quarantine was abolished in December 1953 and personnel of the Division of Forest Insect Investigations were transferred to the various Forest Service Experiment Stations. Those at Coeur d'Alene went to the NRM Station; those at Ogden went to INT; and those at Fort Collins went to the RM Station.

After the Bureau disbanded, Orr went to the SO Station at New Orleans in 1954 and Evenden (at Coeur d'Alene) was briefly FIR Division Chief for the expanded INT (after NRM was combined). He retired on 31 December 1954 and the Coeur d'Alene lab and its personnel (fig. 24) were transferred to Missoula on 31 January 1955. Evenden was replaced by Donald E. Parker, who transferred from the Washington Office. Parker retired in 1966 and Division Chiefs were replaced with Assistant Directors, and Project Leaders came into being. The AD involved with Forest Insect Research was Charles A. (Chuck) Wellner who had been a Silviculturist. Suddenly, Research Entomologists no longer had a line of Entomologists in the administrative chain to Washington. Wellner,

however, had worked in the northern Rocky Mountains throughout his career and that, plus his level-handed administrative style, gained the respect of the FIR staff. That ended with his retirement.

Missoula Forest Insect Laboratory

When Evenden retired in December 1954, the Coeur d'Alene lab was closed, and its personnel were moved to a new Forest Insect Laboratory at Missoula. At this time, personnel included Phillip C. Johnson (Leader succeeding Evenden), Tom Terrell, Archie Gibson, Robert E. Denton, and Galen C. Trostle. Scott Tunnock and David G. Fellin joined them subsequently. Their activities continued to involve the traditional mission of the former Bureau: research, surveys of insect damage, and technical supervision of control projects on federal and other forest ownerships. However, the responsibility for surveys and control supervision was transferred to the respective Forest Service Regions on 1 July 1961. Johnson, Denton, and Fellin continued with INT at Missoula, Gibson retired, and the others went to Region 1. Richard F. Schmitz joined the staff ca 1958 after graduating from Oregon State University where he had been a classmate of Fellin.

Figure 24. Staff of the Coeur d'Alene FIL and Washington Office visitors on a field trip in the Coeur d'Alene National Forest, ID. Front from left: Archie Gibson, James A. Beal, James C. Evenden, and Phillip C. Johnson. Standing: Harvey J. MacAloney, Robert E. Denton, Galen C. Trostle, and Tom T. Terrell (Coeur d'Alene FIL photo by P. C. Johnson).

USDA Forest Service Gen. Tech. Rep. RMRS-GTR-195. 2007

19

After the survey and control functions were transferred to Region 1 (along with Terrell and Tunnock), research mainly involved the western spruce budworm (Fellin), pine engraver beetle (Schmitz), and regeneration insects (Fellin). By his nature, Johnson leaned toward administration, but delved superficially into the budworm and bark beetles. His forte was to accompany and entertain official visitors on field trips. He could recount, in entertaining fashion, the history of whatever subject came to view or mind, whether it be some historical town in the Bitterroot Valley, or some insect outbreak or related study in progress. He was a particularly good photographer, always using a 4 x 5 camera on a tripod and processing and enlarging his film and prints. He faithfully took group pictures of staff meetings and of visitors, several of which are included in this account. His hobby involved trains and he would travel to a commanding place along the Northern Pacific R.R. to photograph a particular train, the schedule of which he knew to the minute. Visitors to his residence were certain to be taken to the basement where he donned a train engineer's hat and operated an elaborate model railroad that duplicated the real thing, including sound effects.

Larch Casebearer

The larch casebearer is native to Eurasia and known to have been accidentally introduced into Massachusetts by 1886. It was discovered in the western US in 1957 by Fellin and Schmitz near St. Maries, ID (Denton 1958). They were driving from Oregon State University to Missoula for summer employment with the Forest Insect Laboratory. On the downgrade south of town, Schmitz asked Fellin what was causing the fade (discoloration) of the western larch foliage. Fellin, who has difficulty perceiving faded foliage, said he didn't see anything wrong. However, they stopped and collected some foliage that had abundant case-bearing caterpillars feeding on the needles. They presented their find to Johnson, who referred to eastern US literature on larch defoliators and thereby identified the insect.

Bob Denton, who had begun study of the larch casebearer on western larch in 1957 while stationed at Missoula, continued with that assignment after his transfer to Moscow. His studies mainly involved use of introduced parasitic wasps, but also included testing non-persistent insecticides. In 1967, he and other members of the Moscow staff documented a nearly total collapse of the needle-mining stage of the casebearer due to extreme hot, dry weather, which desiccated needles containing the fragile young larvae. Aided by this decimation of the population, the various introduced and native parasites gained control and have maintained the casebearer to where it may now be thought of as "naturalized." Even if present, it can only be found by careful scrutiny. I recall Don Parker, who had experience with the casebearer in the eastern US, saying at the start that: "Give it 20 years and it will become naturalized" (under natural control). He missed it by only 10 years too long.

More Reorganization

Unlike the casebearer, ideas for reorganization of forest insect research never subside. In 1961, Forest Service Research was reorganized and the designation "Forest Insect Laboratory" was discontinued and replaced by the "Division of Forest Insect Research" headed by a Division Chief (Donald E. Parker at Ogden) and Research Work Units headed by a Project Leader (Johnson at Missoula). The combined forest insect research personnel at this time are shown in figure 25. Eventually, personnel in disciplines such as forest entomology were absorbed into multi-disciplinary research work units and ecosystem units. As personnel at Missoula gradually retired or transferred, only Fellin remained (assigned

Figure 25. Personnel of INT Division of Forest Insect Research at staff meeting, Missoula, MT, May 3 to 5, 1985. Front row from left: Walter E. Cole, Donald E. Parker, Charles A. Wellner, and David G. Fellin. Back row: Phillip C. Johnson, Richard I. Washburn, Malcolm M. Furniss, Robert E. Denton, and Richard F. Schmitz (Photo #1955 by P. C. Johnson).

to a Silviculture RWU). He retired 3 January 1986, thus becoming the last USDA Research Forest Entomologist stationed in the northern Rocky Mountains since Brunner's appointment in 1909.

Ogden

At various times, INT was within the scope of laboratories at Coeur d'Alene and Fort Collins. However, the area encompassed by the Intermountain Station prior to consolidation with NRM received relatively little attention by Forest Entomologists. Possibly the long traveling distance, perceived lesser importance of the forest resource, and perhaps, less diversity and less severity of forest insect problems, may have accounted for such lack of visitation by Entomologists. This began to change in July 1949 when Leslie W. Orr was transferred to Ogden from the Washington Office of the BE&PQ Division of Forest Insect Investigations. His address was USDA Forest Insect Laboratory, Box 731, Post Office Building. The area assigned to this laboratory coincided with that of the INT, including southern Idaho. He was joined soon thereafter by Richard I. Washburn, who had recently graduated from Colorado State College (now University). Washburn was assigned to activities on the Dixie NF in southern Utah involving the Black Hills beetle in ponderosa pine (fig. 26).

Figure 26. Left to right: J. C. Evenden, L. W. Orr, and R. I. Washburn examining a ponderosa pine infested with Black Hills beetle, Dixie National Forest, UT, 1954. Author photo.

Boise

In 1953, defoliator outbreaks in southern Idaho—coupled with dissolution of BE&PQ and transfer of its FII personnel to the Forest Service and the consolidation of NRM with INT—led to lasting changes in forest entomology at INT. Igniting this change was an outbreak of the pine butterfly in the extensive ponderosa pine stands centered on the Boise NF. In 1954, 169,000 acres were sprayed with DDT under Orr's supervision. This episode, and perhaps consolidation of NRM and INT, elevated entomology into prominence in this area. Additional entomologists were added to the Ogden staff; Walter E. Cole, a recent graduate of Colorado State College, was hired and I transferred from the California Forest and Range Experiment Station, Berkeley, in October 1954.

Also at this time, a vast outbreak of the western spruce budworm occurred on 1 million acres on the Boise NF and four surrounding national forests. Plans were afoot to spray the infestation with DDT. To address these and other insect-related forest management problems, Cole and I were transferred in May 1955 from Ogden to the Boise Research Center on Myrtle Street in Boise, ID. I became the entomologist in charge of the subsequent 1-million acre control project (Furniss 1957), during which I occupied a residence at the administrative site of the Boise Basin Experimental Forest at Idaho City.

In 1956, I was assigned to research on the Douglas-fir beetle and chose a study area on the South Fork of the Salmon River on the Krassel Ranger District, Payette NF. From then until 1963, my family and I spent entire summers in a building constructed by the CCC in the 1930s (fig. 27). The facility had no electricity or phone. My wife, Irene, cooked on a wood stove that also heated water by means of a water pipe leading into the firebox. A wringer washing machine was rigged to operate by a gasoline Briggs & Stratton 4-stroke gasoline engine. Coleman lanterns fueled with white gas provided light. Refrigeration was provided by a Servel (kerosene burner) refrigerator.

Other personnel at Boise Research Center included Robert Ferguson in range research and Joe Basile, a wildlife biologist assigned there by the Idaho Department of Fish and Game. They were trying to determine why bitterbrush was dying or not regenerating on deer winter range in the Payette and Boise River drainages. At a coffee break, I chided them about not including insects in their investigation. I was challenged to participate and, indeed, a stink bug was subsequently found to feed on

USDA Forest Service Gen. Tech. Rep. RMRS-GTR-195. 2007

21

Figure 27. Field quarters for the author's study of the Douglas-fir beetle from 1956 to 1963 at Camp Creek on the South Fork of the Salmon River, ID. Author photo.

bitterbrush seed in the juice stage, drastically lowering its viability (Ferguson and others 1963, Basile and others 1964). Eventually, shrub entomology was made a part of my assigned research and I studied insects on five genera of shrubs in the Northwest. I continued this work on willows in Alaska after retirement, sponsored by Forest Service Region 10, Anchorage.

Cole was assigned to study the western spruce budworm at Boise until transferring back to Ogden to study the mountain pine beetle. He retired there in 1984 and Gene Amman became Project Leader. After Amman retired in 1993, the mountain pine beetle project was relocated to Logan, UT, with Jesse Logan and Barbara Bentz as successive project leaders.

Moscow Forestry Sciences Laboratory 1963 To 1982

In May, 1963, I transferred to the newly built Forestry Sciences Laboratory at Moscow, ID, and enrolled in a graduate study in entomology at University of Idaho under the Government Employees Training Act. For my thesis, I studied the bionomics of a geometrid (looper) defoliator of mountain mahogany on Juniper Mountain, Owyhee County. My major Professor was William F. Barr who, besides being a prominent beetle taxonomist, studied insects of semi-arid-land shrubs. Association with Barr was partly responsible for my interest in

insects of forest-related shrubs important to wildlife and I continued to study them long after retirement.

In 1969, Johnson (at Missoula) retired and a new research work unit, Insects of Northern Rocky Mountain Forest Trees and Wildland Shrubs was established at Moscow. I became Project Leader. Scientific staff consisted of Washburn (spruce budworm), Denton (larch casebearer), and Schmitz (pine engraver beetle).

From 1970 to 1982, I field tested various bark beetle pheromones and discovered the anti-aggregative effect of methylcyclohexenone (MCH) produced by Douglas-fir beetles after mating (Furniss and others 1972). It had been thought by its discoverer, Julius Rudinsky of Oregon State University, to be an attractant. I then conducted a cooperative 10-year research and development project that resulted in a controlled-release formulation (patented) of this pheromone (Furniss and others 1977) and the technology for applying it by helicopter (fig. 28) to prevent populations of beetles from developing in storm-damaged trees where they generate outbreaks (Furniss and others 1981). Region 1 personnel conducted a pilot test of the method in 1982 (McGregor and others 1984). Use of MCH was registered by the EPA in 1999. During the 1970s, other entomologists at Moscow retired (Washburn and Denton) or transferred (Schmitz to Ogden). I retired in April 1982, ending the continuous residence in Idaho of a USDA Research Forest Entomologist since Evenden moved to Coeur d'Alene in the second decade of that century.

22

USDA Forest Service Gen. Tech. Rep. RMRS-GTR-195. 2007

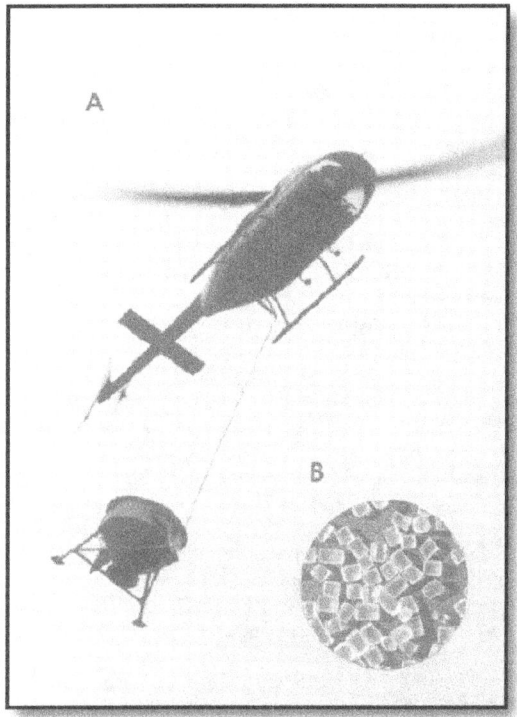

Figure 28. A. Helicopter applying a controlled-release formulation of the Douglas-fir beetle anti-aggregative pheromone, methylcyclohexanone (MCH). B. Inert dimer-polyamine beads containing 2 percent MCH that is eluted over several weeks to prevent beetles from building outbreak populations in wind-felled trees. Author photo.

References Cited

Balch, R. E. 1930. The spruce budworm epidemic on lodgepole in Wyoming. USDA Bur. Entomol. Coeur d'Alene For. Insect Lab. Typed report, 33pp. illus. (Special Collections and Archives Library, Univ. Idaho, Moscow).

Basile, J. V., R. B. Ferguson, and M. M. Furniss. 1964. Six-legged seed eaters. Ida. Wildlife Rev. 17(3):5-7.

Berisford, C. W. 1991. Andrew Delmar Hopkins—a West Virginia pioneer in entomology. W. Va. Univ. Agr. For. Exp. Sta. Cir. 155 (14): 20-26.

Brunner, J. 1909. Tracks and tracking. Ferris Printing Co., NY. Reprinted 1925, Macmillan Co., NY. 219 p.

Brunner, J. 1914. The sequoia pitch moth, a menace to pine in western Montana. USDA Bur. Entomol. Bull. 111. Washington, D.C.

Brunner, J. 1915. Douglas-fir pitch moth. USDA Bur. Entomol. Bull. 255. Washington, D.C.

Burke, H. E. 1946. My recollections of the first years in forest entomology. USDA Bur. Entomol. Plant Quar. Berkeley, CA. (unpublished). Special Collections and Archives Library, Univ. Idaho, Moscow.

Burke, H. E., and B. E. Wickman 1990. Notheastern Oregon bark beetle control project 1910-1911. USDA For. Serv., Pacific Northwest Res. Sta., Gen. Tech. Rep. PNW-GTR-249. Portland, OR.

Denton, R. E. 1958. The larch casebearer in Idaho—a new defoliator record for western forests. U.S. For. Serv. Intermountain. Forest & Range Exp. Sta. Res. Note 51. Ogden, UT.

Denton, R. E. 1959. Unpublished reports by personnel of the Coeur d'Alene Forest Insect Laboratory (1915-1954) and Missoula Forest Insect Lab (1955-1958). USDA, For. Serv. INT, Missoula, MT. A bibliography. Special Collections and Archives Library, Univ. Idaho, Moscow.

Dix, M. E. 1986. Insect research in Great Plains windbreaks. In Current topics in forest research:mphasis on contributions by women scientists. A national symposium, 4-6 November 1986. Gainesville, FL.

Ferguson, R. B., M. M. Furniss, and J. V. Basile. 1963. Insects destructive to bitterbrush flowers and seeds in southwestern Idaho. J. Econ. Entomol. 56:459-462. Ogden, UT.

Furniss, M. M. 1957. Entomological aspects of the 1955 southern Idaho spruce budworm control project. USDA For. Serv. INT For. Range Expt. Sta. Misc. Pub. No. 10. Ogden, UT.

Furniss, M. M. 1967. Nematode parasites of the Douglas-fir beetle in Idaho and Utah. J. Econ. Entomol. 60:1323-1326.

Furniss, M. M. 1997. American forest entomology comes on stage. Bark beetle depredations in the Black Hills Forest Reserve, ca 1897-1907. Amer. Entomol. 4:40-47.

Furniss, M. M. 2003. Forest entomology in the northern Rocky Mountains: 1909-1917, as reflected in the correspondence between Josef Brunner and A. D. Hopkins. Amer. Entomol. 49: 102-111.

Furniss, M. M. 2004. 1947 Douglas-fir tussock moth outbreak in northern Idaho: Target of the largest aerial spraying project in western forests. Latah Legacy. 33 (1):1-8.

Furniss, M. M., and R. Renkin. 2003. Forest entomology in Yellowstone National Park—1922-1957. A time of discovery and learning to let live. Amer. Entomol. 49:198-209.

Furniss, M. M., R. W. Clausen, G. P. Markin, M. D. McGregor, and R. L. Livingston. 1981. Effectiveness of Douglas-fir beetle antiaggregative pheromone applied by helicopter. USDA For. Serv. Gen. Tech. Rep. INT-101. Ogden, UT.

Furniss, M. M., L. N. Kline, R. F. Schmitz, and J. A. Rudinsky. 1972. Tests of three pheromones to induce or disrupt aggregation of Douglas-fir beetles (Coleoptera: Scolytidae) on live trees. Ann. Ent. Soc. Am. 65:1227-1232.

Furniss, M. M., J. W. Young, M. D. McGregor, R. L. Livingston, and D. R. Hamel. 1977. Effectiveness of controlled-release formulations of MCH for preventing Douglas-fir beetle (Coleoptera: Scolytidae) infestation in felled trees. Can. Entomol. 109:1063-1069.

Hopkins, A. D. 1891. Preliminary Report, Black Spruce. West Virginia Agricultural Experiment Station, Bull. 17:93-102.

Hopkins, A. D. 1902. Insect enemies of the pine in the Black Hills Forest Reserve. USDA Div. Entomol. Bull. 32 n.s. Washington, D.C.

Hopkins, A. D. 1905. The Black Hills beetle. USDA Bur. Entomol. Bull. 56. Washington, D.C.

Hopkins, A. D. 1906. Barkbeetle depredations of some fifty years ago in the Pike's Peak region of Colorado. Proc. Entomol. Soc. Wash. VIII: 4, 5.

Keen, F. P. 1939. Insect enemies of western forests. USDA Misc. Public. No. 273. Washington, D.C.

Klade, R. J. 2006. Building a research legacy—The Intermountain Station 1911-1997. Gen. Tech. Rep. RMRS-GTR-184. Fort Collins, CO: U.S. Department of Agriculture, Forest Service, Rocky Mountain Research Station. 259 p.

Larson, R. C. 1979a. Western forest entomology history—Interview of Noel D. Wygant, Fort Collins, CO, 25 March 1979. USDA For. Serv. and For. History Soc., Santa Cruz, CA. (Copy in author's possession).

Larson, R. C. 1979b. Western forest entomology history—Interview of Calvin L. Massey, Albuquerque, NM, 20 March 1979. USDA For. Serv. and For. History Soc., Santa Cruz, CA. (Copy in author's possession).

Larson, R. C. 1979c. Western forest entomology history—Interview of James C. Evenden, Coeur d'Alene, ID, 23 March 1979. USDA For. Serv. and For. History Soc., Santa Cruz, CA. (Edited by M. M. Furniss, 1989, copy in author's possession).

USDA Forest Service Gen. Tech. Rep. RMRS-GTR-195. 2007

23

Massey, C. L. 1956. Nematode parasites and associates of the Engelmann spruce beetle (*Dendroctonus engelmanni* Hopk.). Helminthol. Soc. Washington Proc. 23:14-24.

Massey, C. L. 1974. Biology and taxonomy of nematode parasites and associates of bark beetles in the United States. USDA For. Serv. Agric. Handbook, No. 446. Washington, D.C.

Massey, C. L., and N. D. Wygant. 1954. Biology and control of the Engelmann spruce beetle in Colorado. USDA Circ. 944. Washington, D.C.

Maunder, E. R. 1977. Oral history volume of forest entomology in the west. Interview of F. Paul Keen. Forest History Society and USDA Forest Service. Special Collections, University of Idaho, Moscow.

McCambridge, W. F. 1974. Pinyon needle scale. USDA For. Serv. Pest Leafl. 148. Washington, D.C.

McCambridge, W. F. 1982. Field tests of insecticides to protect ponderosa pine from the mountain pine beetle (Coleoptera: Scolytidae). Jour. Econ. Entomol. 75:1080-1082.

McGregor, M. D. 1970. Biological observations on the life history and habits of *Choristoneura lambertiana* (Lepidoptera: Tortricidae) on lodgepole pine in southeastern Idaho and western Montana. Can. Entomol. 102:1201-1208.

McGregor, M. D., M. M. Furniss, R. D. Oakes, K. E. Gibson, and H. E. Meyer. 1984. MCH pheromone for preventing Douglas-fir beetle infestation in windthrown trees. J. Forestry 82:613-616.

McKnight, M. E. 1971. Biology and habits of *Bracon politiventris* (Hymenoptera: Braconidae). Ann. Entomol. Soc. Amer. 64: 620-624.

McKnight, M. E., and S. Tunnock. 1973. The borer problem in green ash in North Dakota shelterbelts. North Dakota Farm Res. Bimonthly Bull. 30(5):8-14.

Price, R. 1976. History of Forest Service research in the central and southern Rocky Mountain Regions 1908-1975. USDA For. Serv. Gen. Tech. Rep. RM-27. Fort Collins, CO.

Rust, H. J. 1946. Mammals of Northern Idaho. Jour. Mammalogy 27(4):308-327.

Rust, H. J. 1947. Migration and nesting of nighthawks in northern Idaho. The Condor 49(5):177-188.

Sartwell, C., and R. E. Stevens. 1975. Mountain pine beetle in ponderosa pine: prospects for silvicultural control in second-growth stands. J. For. 73:136-140.

Schmid, J. M., and Frye, R. H. 1977. Spruce beetle in the Rockies. USDA For. Serv. Gen. Tech. Report RM-49. Fort Collins, CO.

Schmid, J. M., and Bennett, D. D. 1988. The North Kaibab pandora moth outbreak, 1978-1984. USDA For. Serv. Gen. Tech. Report RM-153. Fort Collins, CO.

Schmid, J. M., and Mata, S. A. 1992. Stand density and mountain pine beetle-caused tree mortality in ponderosa pine stands. USDA For. Serv. Res. Note RM-515. Fort Collins, CO.

Schmid, J. M., and Mata, S. A. 2005. Mountain pine beetle-caused tree mortality in plots surrounded by unmanaged stands. USDA For. Serv. Res. Paper RMRS-RP-54. Fort Collins, CO.

Stevens, R. E., and F. G. Hawksworth. 1984. Insect-dwarf mistletoe relationships: An update. *In* Proc. Biology of dwarf Mistletoes Symposium. F. G. Hawksworth and R. F. Scharpf, coordinators. USDA For. Serv. Gen. Tech. Rept. RM-111. Fort Collins, CO.

Terrell, T. T. 1977. *In* Maunder, E. R. 1977. Oral history volume of forest entomology in the west. Forest History Society and USDA For. Serv. (Special Collections and Archives, Univ. Idaho, Moscow).

Wood, S. L. 1963. A revision of the bark beetle genus *Dendroctonus* Erichson (Coleoptera: Scolytidae). Great. Bas. Nat. 23:1-117.

Wygant, N. D., and A. L. Nelson. 1949. Four billion feet of beetle-killed spruce. USDA Yearbook Agric. 1949. p 417-422. Washington, D.C.

24

USDA Forest Service Gen. Tech. Rep. RMRS-GTR-195. 2007

Appendix A — Fred B. Knight's Recollections of Fort Collins, 1951 to 1960

The person I knew best was Bill Wilford, who was the number 2 man in Fort Collins and the person who worked most closely with people doing spruce beetle control work. He was in charge of spruce beetle surveys, which was my prime assignment along with the mountain pine beetle and general insect problems in the region. Other personnel during my years at Fort Collins (1951 to 1960) included Noel Wygant, in overall charge, who supervised research by Cal Massey, Roy Nagel, Bill McCambridge, and me on surveys working under Wilford. McCambridge was transferred to Juneau, AK, in fall of 1952 (first Forest Entomologist to be stationed there). Frank Yasinski replaced him in Fort Collins.

My research mainly involved insect population sampling and I developed the procedure for sequential sampling of beetle populations. I had additional research responsibilities as well. I was involved in aerial surveys of the spruce beetle and mountain pine beetle, piloted by Robert Heller who was stationed at Beltsville, MD. For many years, I put in a day or two at Mesa Verde going over their lands with the Park people (a fun job). Another nice job was going every year by horseback to inspect insect damage on Missionary Ridge before roads were built. Mountain pine beetle research gave me opportunities to visit most of the ponderosa pine forests of the region. We worked in the Black Hills and the Bighorns (mountains) of Wyoming and throughout Colorado. There was a lot of travel alone in the old green Forest Service panel trucks without a radio to listen to. Radios were allowed about the time I left for Michigan. Those were all wonderful, productive years for me (Fred taught forest entomology at University of Michigan [John Schmid and Gene Amman were among his students] and later at University of Maine. At the time of this writing, he was retired and living in Bangor, ME).

USDA Forest Service Gen. Tech. Rep. RMRS-GTR-195. 2007

25

Appendix B — John M. Schmid's Recollections of Forest Insect Research at the RM Station, 1963 to 1992

Insect Project and Personnel

In 1963, the Forest Insect Research Project at the Rocky Mountain Forest and Range Experiment Station (RM) in Fort Collins, CO, consisted of three Entomologists (Noel Wygant, project leader; William McCambridge; Mel McKnight), one chemist (Roy Nagel), one biological technician (Charles Germain), and a secretary (Judy Dimmick). The project was housed on the second floor of South Hall, a two-storied barracks type building on the CSU campus. At that time, research projects and the administrative staff were housed in various buildings on the CSU campus. South Hall has long since been razed and replaced by the Natural and Environmental Sciences building. The project had laboratory space in one wing of the CSU greenhouse facility, which was located just south of South Hall. In 1967, all RM personnel moved into the new facility on West Prospect Street.

Noel Wygant, Project Leader, worked on the spruce beetle (SB), but was winding down his research in 1963. He was still investigating the effects of temperatures on SB development and the use of cacodylic acid in SB control. Dr. Wygant retired in 1968.

William (Mac) McCambridge worked on the mountain pine beetle (MPB). In the mid-1960s, epidemic MPB populations developed on the Front Range of Colorado. Mac used the infestations to study MPB emergence and attack densities near Allenspark; the effectiveness of protective sprays against the MPB in Lory State Park and the Red Feather Lakes area; MPB response to various "attractants;" and MPB-caused tree mortality in unmanaged stands in Lory State Park.

Simultaneously with his work in the Front Range of Colorado, Mac assisted Bob Heller's Berkeley, CA, remote sensing project in the mid-1960s. Heller's project involved studying the use of thermal imagery and high altitude photography for detecting MPB infestations. The study site was located in the northern Black Hills just east of Terry Peak and in conjunction with the study area of John Schmid. For Christmas 1965, Mac received a subscription to Playboy magazine from an anonymous individual. Mac suspected someone from Heller's crew, most likely Phil Weber or Dick Myhre. During field work one day in the following year, Mac announced that he had not brought a lunch and had to run to town to buy

something to eat. He asked if anyone wanted anything from the store. Dick Myhre responded that he needed a sandwich or something edible, but wasn't real precise. Mac went to town, bought a loaf of bread, some lettuce, and maybe pickles and salad dressing. On the way back to the study area, he stopped in the barnyard on the way to the study area and picked up a cowpie. He placed it between two slices of bread with some lettuce and other items. He gave the "sandwich" to Myhre and when Dick asked what kind of sandwich it was, Mac replied with a straight face "beef." Fortunately for Myhre, he lifted the top slice of bread before biting into the sandwich. After that, a "Big Mac" had a different connotation in the Black Hills!

Mel McKnight worked on the population dynamics of western spruce budworm (WSBW) populations in Colorado and New Mexico. His research concentrated on survival/mortality of the different life stages with emphasis on the role of insect parasites on WSBW population levels. His research culminated in a Ph.D. dissertation in 1967 titled "Ecology of the western budworm, *Choristoneura occidentalis* Freeman (Lepidoptera: Torticidae), in Colorado." Mel transferred to the Shelterbelt Laboratory in Bottineau, ND, in 1968 to work on shelterbelt insects. Mel worked on shelterbelt insects until 1973 when he transferred to WO and became one of the coordinators for the joint Canada-United States Spruce Budworms Program (CANUSA).

Roy Nagel worked on the spruce beetle. He tested chemicals for their effectiveness against the spruce beetle, tagged beetles with radioactive chemicals to follow their direction and distance of dispersal, and collaborated with others on the development of the trap tree method for reducing SB populations. Roy retired in 1966 and was replaced by J. M. Schmid.

Roy's reputation for playing practical jokes was well known among his associates. One of his favorite tricks was to place a cerambycid or cockroach in a small metal aspirin container, the type that aspirin tablets were sold in during the 1960s. He would carry the container in his pocket. When eating in a restaurant, he would order coffee. After the waitress had delivered the coffee and he had drunk a portion of it, he would remove the insect from the container and place it in the remaining coffee. He would then holler for the waitress and after she returned to the table, begin to berate her with comments about the cleanliness of the establishment and/or the quality of the food. Eventually, he received additional free coffee and/or a free meal. If he received a Roosevelt dime in change while paying his bill, he would throw it back at the cashier because he hated Roosevelt.

Roy was also known for spending time on non-entomological activities when on field trips. According to Don Lucht, former Entomologist with Forest Insect and Disease Management (FIDM) in Albuquerque, Roy and Don traveled to the vicinity of Lizard Head pass near Telluride, CO, in 1954 to check on background levels of radiation in the forest. Because the US had recently exploded an atomic bomb, radioactive fallout from the explosion had increased the radiation levels in the forest to the point that background radiation levels were well above what would be normally expected. Rather than cancel their field work because of the radiation threat and return immediately to Fort Collins, they jokingly said that they spent most of the time looking for "two-headed railroad spikes" along the narrow gauge railroad tracks in the area.

Chuck Germain assisted the entomologists in their various projects. He was an accomplished guitarist and regularly played at various locations in the Cheyenne-Fort Collins-Denver area on the weekends. He transferred to the FIDM unit in Albuquerque, NM, in 1967.

Jim Mitchell replaced Germain as the project's technician. He worked for various members of the project in Fort Collins, but was primarily assigned to work with Schmid during the 1970s. He conducted the SB solar heat study in the summers of 1970 and 1971, and a study on seed and cone insects of Engelmann spruce from 1974 to 1977. When the project was terminated in 1981, he was offered a job in Flagstaff, AZ, and accepted it.

Steve Mata (see Appendix D) was hired as a Biological Technician in 1964 to work with McKnight on WSBW research. After McKnight transferred to Bottineau in 1968, Mata was assigned to work with Mac until 1981 when the insect project was terminated. He then worked with Stevens and others until Stevens retired in 1983. Thereafter, Mata worked exclusively with Schmid, who retired in 1992. After Schmid retired, Mata became a Forestry Technician and worked with Wayne Shepperd until 2005. Mata retired in June 2005 upon completing 40 years service with the Rocky Mountain Station. Despite being assigned to various supervisors and lines of work during his career, Steve maintained a high-level

of performance and became well-versed in bark beetle ecology and management, data analysis via computers, and management of studies assigned to him.

Bob Stevens replaced Noel Wygant as Project Leader in 1968, transferring to Fort Collins from the Washington Office. Stevens was project leader until the project was terminated in 1981. He was then offered a position in the multifunctional project in Fort Collins, which was headed by Bob Alexander. He worked on that project until he retired in 1983.

Pam Farrar joined the project as a Biological Technician in May 1976. She worked with Schmid on insects associated with sagebrush on the Stratton Experimental Watershed west of Saratoga, WY, on WSBW parasites in chemically treated and non-treated areas in northern New Mexico, and on the distribution of foliage on white fir and Douglas-fir. When the project was terminated in 1981, she was offered a position in Lincoln, NE. She declined the offer and accepted an Administrative Assistant position in fiscal at Station headquarters in Fort Collins. She continued in that position until October 1982 when she accepted a Biological Technician position with the wildlife project (Effects of multiple-use management on wildlife in the Central Rocky Mountains) in Laramie, WY.

In 1981, the insect project in Fort Collins was terminated. Stevens and Mata were offered positions in a multifunctional project in Fort Collins and both accepted. McCambridge and Farrar were offered positions in Lincoln, NE, but both declined the offers. McCambridge remained in Fort Collins for another year to finish manuscripts on studies he had completed and then retired. Farrar accepted a position in fiscal at station headquarters. Mitchell and Schmid were offered positions in Flagstaff, AZ. Both accepted the offers and transferred to Flagstaff in 1981/1982.

Although entomological research as a separate project in Fort Collins ended with the termination of the insect project, some research continued as part of Alexander's multifunctional project. In addition, entomological research was incorporated with Frank Hawkworth's pathology project when it became a disease-insect impact project in the mid-1980s.

Personal Account

I began work as a temporary summer employee at RM in Fort Collins in the summer of 1963 through the efforts of Fred Knight. Dr. Knight worked at RM as a research entomologist from 1950 to 1960 and resigned

USDA Forest Service Gen. Tech. Rep. RMRS-GTR-195. 2007

27

from the RM Station in 1960 to become professor of forest entomology in the School of Natural Resources at the University of Michigan. Dr. Knight maintained contact with his former associates at RM and when the insect project planned to hire temporary workers, he was contacted to see if he had any prospective candidates for the summer work. I was fortunate to be one of his students in 1963 and to be recommended for the job.

The position was primarily to assist McCambridge in his studies on the MPB. However, McKnight needed assistance with his WSBW work in the initial part of the summer so I traveled with him to northern New Mexico to sample WSBW populations. After that, I worked with McCambridge on MPB. I spent time in late July and early August checking emergence cages and determining the location and rates of MPB attacks on ponderosa pine near Allenspark, CO. In addition, I came to RM hoping I could gather data during the summer, which to use for a graduate degree. At the time, the project focused on why some MPB-attacked trees were unsuccessfully attacked, i.e., trees were attacked but not killed. Thinking at that time centered around anatomical differences in the trees and the possibility that unsuccessfully attacked trees may have greater numbers of resin canals than successfully attacked trees. When not working for McCambridge, I was allowed to search for unsuccessfully-attacked trees and take increment cores from them and adjacent successfully-attacked trees. I took the cores back to the U. of Michigan.

In 1964, I returned to the RM Station in Fort Collins for another summer of employment and worked with McKnight on his WSBW parasite studies. Except for field trips to locations in Colorado to collect WSBW larvae and pupae, I worked most of the summer in McKnight's trailer lab rearing budworms and their parasites. The larvae were constantly supplied fresh foliage and parasite cocoons were removed and placed in separate containers as they appeared. The cocoons were maintained until the adults emerged. Eventually, the adults were identified and levels of parasitism were determined for each species.

My reasons for returning in 1964 were to present Dr. Wygant with my thesis and to see if the project would finance a study for another graduate degree. After consultation with other project personnel, he agreed to finance another study.

During the 1964/1965 school year at Michigan, I selected the topic of parasites and predators of the MPB for my graduate degree. I returned to Fort Collins in May 1965 and began work on the study. Initially, locating a suitable study area became the first priority. Bill Bailey, aerial survey specialist with FIDM in Lakewood, CO, was familiar with MPB infestations on the Roosevelt NF and agreed to show them to me. We journeyed up the Poudre Canyon and stopped near Washout Gulch to examine a spot uphill. When we left the vehicle, we walked through sagebrush and other brush on the lower slopes. We stopped to rest part way up the slope and as Bill leaned against a rock, I told Bill he'd better check his pants as he had two ticks on one pantleg. He spotted them and then began to laugh. He said you better examine your own pants, John. As I looked down, I saw 10 ticks, five on each leg. Fortunately, that site was not suitable for the study.

After examining a number of locations near Estes Park, Poudre Canyon, and Red Feather Lakes, I reported to Dr. Wygant that I had been unable to locate a suitable area. He asked Mac to take me to the Black Hills because epidemic MPB populations existed in the northern Hills in 1965. We went to the Black Hills in June 1965 and eventually located a suitable study area east of Terry Peak in the exemption area. The area is pictured in figure 214 in Furniss and Carolin's book, Western Forest Insects (1977). Mac was working on MPB responses to various chemicals (attractants) in the laboratory in 1965. He used large numbers of MPB in the tests and was always obtaining beetle-infested bolts whenever possible. As we left the Hills during our scouting trip, we stopped along Highway 85 just east of O'Neil Pass to cut an infested tree. I reached to take the chainsaw out of the truck but Mac said "Let me have the chainsaw, let the old Alaskee (Alaska vet) logger show you how." For those unfamiliar with Mac, he had worked in southern Alaska before working in the central Rockies. Mac proceeded to cut the tree and, in his words, hung that tree to a "fair-thee-well." He cut bolts off the base of the tree but no amount of bolt removal shook the tree loose. Instead, it just became entangled in the other trees and the stem became more vertical so that when we left it, the tree looked like the crown started at ground-level. I always get a chuckle when I drive by that location!

For the remainder of the summer of 1965 and May through September in 1966 and 1967, I worked on the study area east of Terry Peak. I spent the days taking bark samples for counts of MPB and associated insects as well as observing insect predators operating on the infested trees. Occasionally, I helped Heller's crew with their studies by periodically photographing infested trees to determine changes in their foliage color, and caught a ride with Bill Bailey during his annual survey of insect conditions in the Black Hills. Changes in my employment status and line of research occurred in 1966 and 1967. Roy Nagel retired in 1966 and I was selected to replace him. Upon completion of my third field season in the Black Hills in 1967, I terminated the study and worked on data analysis and preparation of the thesis. Project research at that time was concentrated on the MPB, SB, and WSBW. Because Dr. Wygant was reducing his research on the SB, and Mac and Mel were working on the MPB and WSBW respectively, I was assigned to begin work on the SB in late 1967.

SB research from 1968 to 1977 concentrated on SB populations in logging residuals and blowdown, SB mortality in cull logs caused by solar heat, development of spruce-fir stands following SB outbreaks, the use of Silvisar 510 to control SB populations, and needle temperatures of SB-infested trees. The SB research was thus a mix of long- and short-term studies, so different studies were conducted simultaneously. This work culminated in a comprehensive publication (Schmid and Frye 1977). Intermixed with the SB studies was work on the roundheaded pine beetle in New Mexico in 1970 to 1972, seed and cone insects of Engelmann spruce at the Fraser Experimental Forest in Colorado from 1974 to 1978, and insects associated with sagebrush in the Stratton Experimental Watershed west of Saratoga, WY, from 1972 to 1974.

Project funding was slowly declining in the late 1970s. As a result, the project sought additional funding from the 1977 Canada-United States Spruce Budworms Research and Development Program (CANUSA) to supplement dwindling resources. After the departure of McKnight in 1968, no significant research had been done on the WSBW. Stevens and I submitted proposals that were funded. My CANUSA-funded work included: a study of the effect of aerial spraying on WSBW parasites (1977 to 1979), distribution of foliage on white fir and Douglas-fir (1979), and the distribution of WSBW parasites on white fir and Douglas-fir (1978 to 1979).

In 1979, a major pandora moth infestation was detected on the North Kaibab, AZ. Working around the WSBW investigations, several studies were initiated on the pandora moth. Pupal-inhabited sites were burned in 1980 to determine if prescribed burning could be used to reduce pandora moth populations. Larval populations were sampled in 1981 to determine their distribution on host trees.

The insect project was terminated in 1981. I was offered a position in Flagstaff, AZ, and transferred there in 1982. The research assignment was to determine the influence of seed and cone insects on production of ponderosa pine seed although neither I nor other project personnel had heard that seed and cone insects of ponderosa pine in Arizona were considered an important research priority.

Fortunately for me, the pandora moth epidemic continued on the North Rim of the Grand Canyon on the Kaibab NF. While studies on seed and cone insects were initiated in 1984, I spent more of my time on the North Kaibab following the pandora moth epidemic. In cooperation with Dayle Bennett, Terry Rogers, and Iral Ragenovich of Forest Pest Management from Region 3, information was derived on: distribution of egg masses, first instar larvae and larval populations, emergence of moths, growth impact of defoliation, and the effectiveness of several insecticides. The information was summarized in Schmid and Bennett (1988).

In 1984, I transferred back to Fort Collins and replaced Stevens as the entomologist in Alexander's multifunctional project. The research assignment was to determine the relationship between stand density and MPB-caused tree mortality through the installation of sets of plots, usually four plots to a set with three cut to different stocking levels (GSLs) and the fourth left uncut to serve as the control. With the able assistance of Steve Mata, sets of plots were installed in northern Colorado on the Arapaho-Roosevelt NF, Routt NF, and Colorado State Forest; in southern Wyoming on the Medicine Bow NF; and on the Black Hills NF in SD. After installation, the plots were monitored for MPB activity. Partial cutting to GSLs of less than 80 sq. ft basal area per acre reduced MPB-caused tree mortality in ponderosa pine stands (Schmid and Mata 1992), although this treatment may be less effective if only a small area is cut within an otherwise uncut stand (Schmid and Mata 2005). Stands partially cut to GSLs between 80 and 110 may also be less susceptible but may grow rather quickly to susceptible thresholds. Hopefully, research will follow the plots in the future because significant information on MPB management can be gained.

Additional studies were undertaken on some sets of plots after installation was completed. Bark temperature (1989 to 1992), air movement (1989), moisture stress (1986 to 1988), and verbenone depletion rate (1991) studies were performed on various sets of plots. In conjunction with Gene Amman, INT, and Ken Lister, FPM Region 2, verbenone studies were conducted in Colorado and South Dakota during the summers of 1988 and 1989. In 1992, I retired from RM but continue to periodically monitor the GSL plots in the Black Hills and Wyoming. During my years at RM, I received assistance and support from the FIDM crews from Region 2 and 3; National Forest personnel from the forests in AZ, CO, NM, SD, and WY; the Colorado State Forest Service; and employees at RM/RMRS. In particular, Noel Wygant, Bill McCambridge, and Steve Mata made significant contributions to my research and productivity.

Although I worked extensively on the MPB and SB, my favorite insect to study was the pandora moth. While bark beetles cause extensive tree mortality on landscape levels that are conspicuously visible, the beetles themselves are seldom found outside the bark of trees and are rarely seen. The pandora moth, in contrast, is relatively large in all stages and easily seen. During the epidemic on the North Kaibab NF, adults would swarm at night around the outside lights at the Jacob Lake Inn. Literally thousand of moths could be seen. In the morning, their bodies littered the parking area near the entrance to the Inn and a sound similar to popping popcorn could be heard when cars drove over their bodies. Some adults became flightless because they lost the scales on their wings while constantly fluttering around the lights at night. One crawled up my pant leg one evening while I was seated near the entrance. That epidemic was truly impressive.

I was fortunate to work in most of the Rocky Mountain states, but mainly in the southern and central Rockies and the Black Hills. Of all the places I worked, my favorite place was the Black Hills. The Hills had ample MPB populations, an active timber program for MPB management (at least when I worked there), significant historical events, and scenic/cultural attractions. The time spent in the Hills was both professionally and personally rewarding. In essence, my research career began and ended in the Hills.

Appendix C — Melvin E. McKnight's
Recollections of the RM Station, 1959 to 1973

My experiences with the USDA Forest Service and the Rocky Mountain Forest and Range Experiment Station began on May 5, 1959 when I was reassigned from USDA Agricultural Research Service (ARS), Entomology Research Division. I had entered Federal service exactly 1 year 11 months earlier, at the end of my first year of graduate work in the Department of Entomology at the University of Nebraska in Lincoln. My first professional position had been at the Forage Insect Laboratory in Lincoln evaluating mechanisms of resistance in alfalfa to the spotted alfalfa aphid.

Instead of "going through the line" at graduation for my Master's degree in 1958, Maria and I took a week's vacation in Estes Park, CO. For us, having come from forested Vermont, the mountains and the possibility of moving westward had a lot of appeal. My supervisor at the time, Dr. Wayne L. Howe, reminded me that the Rocky Mountain Station had a research unit in the Plant Sciences Building where the Department of Entomology was housed (Wayne worked with Cal Massey for a summer in Colorado). Dr. Ralph Read, the leader of that unit, told me that RM Station had a vacant position for a Survey Entomologist in Fort Collins. I applied for the position, interviewed, was accepted, and the reassignment from ARS to Forest Service was arranged. At the time, ARS, at least in the Entomology Research Division, encouraged young scientists to move around quite often, every 2 or 3 years, to gain experience. Alternatives presented to me included Bakersfield, CA (alfalfa insects), Tifton, GA (field crop insects), and Cuba (rice insects) (Fidel Castro was still in the mountains!). Obviously, the mountains and forest insects had more appeal!

Dr. Noel Wygant, Chief, Division of Forest Insect Research, and Dr. Bill H. Wilford, Leader, Forest Insect Laboratory, took quite a risk in accepting me for the position. Or perhaps, it was in desperation as the position had been vacant for some time and the field season was rapidly approaching! I believe my predecessors had been Ken Stewart and H. Eugene Ostmark. As I recall, both had left the Forest Service—Ostmark for the United Fruit Company in Honduras. I had no forestry in my undergraduate studies in agronomy at the University of Vermont and only occasional reference to forest insects in my graduate classes at Nebraska. However, I did have a strong background and academic record in entomology at the graduate level and much interest in working outside in the forest environment.

The responsibility of the Forest Insect Laboratory was forest insect research and, in cooperation with Forest Service Region 2, forest insect surveys and pilot control projects in Colorado and Wyoming. Bill Wilford was in charge and was my supervisor. Amel Landgraf did the aerial surveys. I was to do ground surveys with Amel. Dr. Fred B. Knight was studying bark beetle biology and methods of sampling their abundance. Roy H. Nagel researched chemical methods of control. These good people took me from the world of corn and alfalfa insects to the world of bark beetles and defoliators.

My first summer, 1959, was a wonderful experience. I traveled throughout the Region, usually with Amel and occasionally with Bill, inspecting and sampling bark beetle and defoliator infestations. We usually traveled with a complete camping outfit and seldom used commercial lodging, choosing instead to camp by the road or by a fishable stream, and sometimes in a national Forest Guard Station or on the floor in a Ranger Station. Per diem rates were perhaps $6 or $8, less for our summer assistants. In 1959, John C. Nord was our summer assistant on surveys. Later Nord spent most of his career as a research entomologist in the Southeastern Forest Experiment Station. John Chansler and Daniel T. Jennings were assistants of Fred Knight and Roy Nagel. John served in many locations in his career in forest pest management. Dan became a Research Entomologist working with Dr. Calvin Massey at Albuquerque. In 1976, Dan transferred to the Northeast Station to work on spruce budworm research at Orono, ME, where Fred Knight was Dean of the College of Forest Resources at the University of Maine. In 1988, Dan and I were co-authors, with Susan Hacker and Fred Knight, of "North American Coniferophagous *Choristoneura*: A Bibliography." Dan is still active in research as an authority on taxonomy of spiders.

As the newest and most junior member of the group, care and maintenance of the laboratory's insect collection became my responsibility. I became acquainted with the Hopkins US System of recording collection data and biological information on forest insect specimens

USDA Forest Service Gen. Tech. Rep. RMRS-GTR-195. 2007

31

collected during studies and other activities. I maintained an interest in the Hopkins System for the remainder of my career and beyond.

I don't recall what sampling method we used in 1959 for the spruce budworm, *Choristoneura fumiferana*, (later determined to be the "western spruce budworm," *C. occidentalis*). By 1960, the protocols developed at the Pacific Northwest Station by Carolin and Coulter specified that the foliage from one side of each of two branches cut from the mid-crowns of five Douglas-fir trees per sample plot would be examined to obtain counts of budworm egg masses of the current year and previous year to arrive at a ratio suggesting the population trend. Climbing trees and examining a lot of foliage rather quickly led us to think about the feasibility and validity of using smaller samples taken from the ground with pole pruners. This later became an element of my research assignment.

In 1960 and/or 1961, our budworm survey was headquartered at the Del Norte Ranger Station, Rio Grande NF. John Braidwood and Joe Zimmer were summer assistants helping with foliage collections. Four wives of District personnel were the foliage examining crew and Bill Wilford made the egg mass determinations.

On October 1, 1961, I was placed on Military Furlough. The Colorado National Guard unit, Company B of the 140th Signal Battalion (Combat Area), of which I was a member (Area Communication Chief), was activated in response to the Berlin Crisis. I returned to a position with the RM Station on August 13, 1962.

About this time, 1961 or 1962, a significant reorganization in the Forest Service occurred. Responsibilities for forest insect (and disease) surveys were reassigned to the Regions. Consequently, Bill Wilford and Amel Landgraf left the Station for Region 2 in Denver (Amel may have left earlier). Also about this time, Fred Knight left the Forest Service and the Station for the University of Michigan and Bill McCambridge filled the bark beetle position. Noel Wygant was now our Project Leader.

When I returned from military duty, I found myself assigned to research on the budworm. A laboratory trailer had been designed and built for this work. While I was gone, John Schmid had begun studies involving

rearing-out parasites of the budworm from various locations. Robert Dalleske, a graduate student at Colorado State University, was also involved and developed his Master's thesis on budworm parasites. For the 1963 season, the trailer remained parked at Fort Collins. John Schmid continued to assist in the budworm work as did Tom Borg, a student from Colorado State University. Some time later, two Biological Technician positions were made available for budworm research. Steve Mata (fig. 29) and Gilbert Olivas filled these positions. Steve worked in support of forest insect research at the Station for his entire career. Eventually, the lab trailer and a small camper trailer for the technicians were moved to the San Isabel Ranger Station, San Isabel NF.

Figure 29. Steve Mata checking spruce budworm emergence from Douglas-fir samples during study of over-wintering larvae, 1965 (Fort Collins photo FC-634 by M. E. McKnight).

About this time, the massive research effort, "the Green River Project," of the Canadian Forestry Service on the spruce budworm in New Brunswick became well known. The body of work summarized by R.F. Morris in 1963 became the guidance for many scientists studying population dynamics of forest insects. It was made clear that my research on the western budworm in Colorado was to take the same direction on a microscale. Although I was quite unprepared to undertake research largely based on mathematical modeling of population dynamics, we did accumulate meaningful information in life tables for several budworm populations on the San Isabel National Forest. Although our cooperators in pest management in Regions 2 and 3 understood the importance of knowledge of budworm population dynamics, they were especially interested in development of more efficient budworm sampling methods. Thanks to an excellent cooperative relationship with the entomologists in Region 2, I was able to incorporate work on sampling methods with the life table work. Most of my work on the western budworm became my Ph.D. dissertation (1967) at Colorado State University, Department of Zoology. With this summary in hand, and western budworm populations and damage at a relatively low level, the Region 2 entomologists advised the Station that budworm research should not be given high priority.

In 1963, *Bracon politiventris*, normally rare, was abundant in some areas and suspected of being the final factor in eliminating budworm populations in some specific locations. My laboratory and field studies of its life history and habits were not included in the dissertation but were published in McKnight (1971).

Another area of research I would have liked to pursue was to study, at the cellular level, the supposedly obligate diapause of the budworm. I found that second-instar budworm larvae, removed from their hibernacula and placed on suitable food, would feed and develop normally without the period of cold treatment usually considered necessary to eventually "break" diapause. This observation encouraged me to think that the mechanism of diapause in the budworm was an area worthy of study. However, the nature of that research was certainly outside the mission of the project.

Coincidentally, about this time a reorganization of geographic responsibilities of Forest Service Experiment Stations resulted in the Shelterbelt Laboratory at Bottineau, ND, being transferred from the North Central Experiment Station to the Rocky Mountain Station (as mentioned above, a well-established RM Station research unit already existed at Lincoln, NE, that focused on problems in Great Plains forestry). The North Central Station had conducted some basic survey work on insect problems in northern Plains tree plantings and nurseries and staffed a permanent position at the Shelterbelt Laboratory. John D. Stein was in that position. I was offered the position of Project Leader to establish a new project on "Biology, ecology, and control of insects in the Great Plains." I accepted the position and my reassignment was effective April 21, 1968.

The move to Bottineau was less traumatic and the Plains environment less foreign to my wife and me than perhaps it would have been to other Forest Service entomologists.

We had lived in Lincoln, NE, 1956 to 1959 while I was in graduate school and working for ARS. Part of my active duty military time had been spent at Fort Riley, KS. We liked the openness of the Great Plains and we appreciated their historical importance in the development of our country. We were quite comfortable in the small town environment of about 2,500 people. The Shelterbelt Laboratory was on the campus of the North Dakota School of Forestry (later North Dakota State University-Bottineau Branch), one of the oldest forestry schools in the nation. The North Dakota Forest Service was also located at NDSU.

The other project at the Shelterbelt Laboratory was a timber management project headed by Paul Slabaugh, Silviculturist. Paul worked for many years in the Great Plains and was a wealth of information on all aspects of selection, care, and maintenance of trees and tree plantings in the harsh environments the width and breadth of the Plains. Other scientists in that project were Richard Tinus, Tree Physiologist, and Richard Cunningham, Geneticist.

I came to the project with good background knowledge of Forest Service Research documentation. At the outset, there was a need to implement the work unit description, develop problem analyses and study plans, and push forward with publications. I also had good working relationships with the pest management people in Regions 1 and 2. Those units had responsibilities for evaluating pest conditions on the Plains. Over time, we developed the interests of entomologists in both Regions and traveled together extensively looking at insect problems in the Plains.

As the Project Leader of a newly organized research effort, I had to develop contacts with a broad array of cooperators and clients in universities, state forestry agencies, Extension Service, Soil Conservation Service, Soil Conservation Districts, Agricultural Research Service, etc. As our interests and responsibilities became known, we developed cooperative efforts with several institutions and agencies.

Early on it became important to clarify the research role of the project with respect to the expectations of some of our cooperators. The mission of the project was to develop means of detecting, evaluating, and controlling insects with damage potential. Tools were provided for the action agencies. We did not have authority or means to perform the actual work of detecting, evaluating, and controlling pests. Further, it was necessary to focus attention on insects of greatest damage potential. More

USDA Forest Service Gen. Tech. Rep. RMRS-GTR-195. 2007

33

than 300 species of insects had been collected from trees and shrubs used in protective plantings. Only a few had been serious problems, but many more had potential for serious damage.

There seemed to be a poor understanding in Forest Service Research of the importance of our research assignment. The concept of insect-caused impacts on protective tree plantings is quite different than impacts of forest insects on National Forests and commercial forest lands. The justification of our research was to reduce insect-caused losses of windbarrier effectiveness, esthetics, wildlife food and shelter, highway safety and beauty, noise abatement, and invested dollars. Millions of dollars have been invested in the plantings in the Plains. Unlike the situation in most public and private forest lands, every tree and shrub in protective plantings has a dollar value derived from the costs of propagation, planting, and care. We cited information that in 1968, $1,000,000 was reimbursed to farmers in the ASCS program in the Northern, Central, and Southern Plains for conservation practices involving planting trees and shrubs. These were taxpayers' dollars, a public investment that warranted protection.

For the new project, Jack Stein and I were blessed with generous funding for supplies and equipment for our laboratories and field work. We invested in high-quality photographic equipment, and we equipped the lab's darkroom. We were able to hire summer assistants for the field seasons. The project was allocated a full-time technician position. Arden Tagestad was hired for that position and continued to support the work until the project was moved to Lincoln sometime after 1973.

Jack Stein was an observant and enthusiastic collector of insects. He was especially talented at developing guides and keys to identify insects and damage, working tools much needed at the beginning of the project. I also did a lot of collecting, especially using portable Malaise traps, some in place for a few days, some providing periodic collections over the full season. I was particularly interested in the parasitic Hymenoptera from those "forested prairie environments," saved the Braconidae for our insect collection at Bottineau, and sent the Ichneumonidae to John Schmid at Fort Collins. We had good laboratory and greenhouse facilities so we all did a lot of rearing out of collected material. For example, I arranged for collections from many locations, some as far south as Texas, from which we reared pine tip moths to better define the taxonomic status of these important pests of pine plantings. We cooperated with other scientists, including Dan Jennings, testing sex attractants for pine tip moths and other insects including the ash or lilac borer. Through our work we added many new host and locality records for insects of trees and shrubs and their natural enemies as reported in our publications and those of our cooperators.

There was good information dating back to early work in the 1930s that borers were important pests of tree plantings. In the new project, we made a special effort to focus on the borers of green ash, an important species in single- and multi-row shelterbelts. With excellent cooperation of entomologists from Region 1, we were able to get a good quantitative evaluation of borer problems in green ash plantings in North Dakota shelterbelts. In cooperation with the North Dakota Agricultural Experiment Station, we produced a publication (McKnight and Tunnock 1973) that defined the historical problem, the situation in 1972, and an approach to reduce the impact of borers through surveillance, detection, and suppression. Related to this work, in 1970 we began a series of demonstrations, completed after I left the Shelterbelt Lab, showing that borer infestations could be significantly reduced in field shelterbelts using chemical insecticides. These results were also published by the North Dakota Experiment Station to reach the target audiences.

In August, 1973, I was reassigned to a Staff Assistant position for Forest Insect Research in the Forest Insect and Disease Research Staff, in the Forest Service Washington Office. Dr. Mary Ellen Dix was hired to fill the vacant position at the Shelterbelt Laboratory in Bottineau. When the Rocky Mountain Station closed the laboratory at Bottineau in 1983, Jack Stein was transferred to the Pacific Southwest Station and an assignment in Hawaii. Mary Ellen Dix was reassigned to the RM Station laboratory in Lincoln, Nebraska where she published a comprehensive and impressive review of accomplishments of Great Plains insect research (Dix 1986).

Reflections

In 1959, Colorado State University had about 5,000 students. The Rocky Mountain Station offices were at various locations on campus. The Director and headquarters staff, including Noel Wygant, Director of Forest Insect Research and Lake Gill, Director of Forest Disease Research, were housed in the Forestry Building. The Forest Insect Laboratory, and the Forest Disease Laboratory with Dr. Frank Hawksworth and Tommy Hinds, was in South Hall, a two-story, multi-winged former military

34

USDA Forest Service Gen. Tech. Rep. RMRS-GTR-195. 2007

barracks. The new Station building was built on the south edge of campus and occupied in 1967.

≈

I first met Cal Massey when I was traveling with Bill Wilford. We were in Durango, CO, probably collecting foliage for the budworm survey. For some reason, Cal was to come up from Albuquerque and meet Bill at the Strater Hotel where we were staying. When we settled ourselves in the lobby to wait for Cal, Bill told me to watch for a fellow with red hair, red face, and smoking a cigar. After a long evening, Cal eventually appeared, true to Bill's description. Certainly his language was colorful and he was irreverent, yes, but I'm sure it was a tough and continuing battle to justify and garner support for pioneering research that many considered "impractical."

In the mid-1960s, Federal Employees were encouraged to buy United States Savings Bonds through payroll deductions. Allegedly, Cal would "threaten" his employees with "Bonds or (be sent to) Bottineau!" Those who didn't know better considered Bottineau to be an undesirable location. Even though I bought bonds, I went to Bottineau!

I did not have the pleasure of working with Massey in Fort Collins or Albuquerque. I was pleased. however, to have him visit us in Bottineau. He named a nematode, *Omemeea maxbassiensis* n. gen., n. sp., for the location near Bottineau where he found it in the galleries of *Leperisinus californicus*, a bark beetle in green ash and the subject of a study with our cooperator at NDSU-Bottineau. This is another example demonstrating that the northern Great Plains is fertile ground for biological investigation.

≈

Bill Wilford (fig. 30) was the best supervisor and mentor of my career, and a dear friend. I learned much from him, the least of which was forest entomology. Bill was a rigorous editor. My draft reports came back bleeding from his red-pencil treatment. He insisted on correct information, proper English, and clear and understandable writing. We traveled together often and it was always a pleasure. I remember many a beautiful Colorado morning driving down the highway and musing "Not a cloud in the sky!" Almost invariably Bill took the challenge and eventually found a wisp of a cloud I had missed. A stickler for detail! In the field, Bill insisted on doing his share and more of whatever the task at hand, including climbing the big Douglas-fir on the San Juan NF.

The last time we saw Bill was at our home in Bottineau. Jack Stein, Arden Tagestad, and I drove up to Edmonton, Alberta for the Western Forest Insect Work Conference. Bill was in attendance, having driven up from Colorado in his Nash Metropolitan. After the meetings, we left for home; Bill was to follow some hours later. It was a typically cold, blustery drive with whiteouts of wind-driven snow. Somewhere along the route we stopped for coffee and there were a couple of RCMP officers also in the shop. When we left, we commented to the troopers that they might watch for an older gentlemen with a little car. Later, when Bill got to our house, he said he felt quite safe along that long route because he saw so many RCMP vehicles. I don't believe he ever knew that we had arranged his escort!

We last talked to Bill in Easton, Pennsylvania, which he apparently considered "home." (I believe for his entire career he kept his bank accounts in Easton!) We were on the way to Vermont for a visit, found a phone booth near Easton, got his phone number, and called. We suggested going to see him, even for a few minutes. He asked us not to do so. We suspect he was quite ill. He died not long thereafter (he died in 1973 at the home of his son, Tom, in Fort Collins).

Figure 30. Bill Wilford. Photo provided by M. E. McKnight.

USDA Forest Service Gen. Tech. Rep. RMRS-GTR-195. 2007

35

Roy Nagel was a salty ex-Marine. I never worked with Roy in the field, but it is my impression he was a meticulous scientist insistent on documentation of details and observations. He took the time to teach me a lot about photography with his beloved Leica system and darkroom techniques. I think he appreciated my background in entomology more than did some other colleagues. In 1968, I was honored to receive the gift of his "Imms" (Recent Advances in Entomology, A.D. Imms) inscribed on the flyleaf, "R.H. Nagel, Grad. School, U. of Minn., 5/20/34."

I have few recollections of Noel Wygant. His office was in the Forestry Building until the reorganization and move to the new RM Station building. Surely my transfer from ARS to the Forest Service and the Station was with his approval, and for that I am most thankful. I believe he felt that reassignment to shelterbelt insect research, his interest of long-standing, was appropriate and in my best interest. I remember an expression he used fairly often, "That's just the thing we are trying to avoid!" when an idea or suggestion came up in a project staff meeting.

Arden Tagestad was the best technician I had the pleasure to work with in my career. He was a North Dakota farm boy with a family of several young children. He had been employed as a part-time or seasonal employee, perhaps as an equipment operator, with the local Soil Conservation District. He was happy to fill our permanent position as biological technician in support of the shelterbelt research project. With our encouragement, he took one or more entomology courses at North Dakota State University-Bottineau Branch and followed up with study on his own. He was a keen observer in the field and in the laboratory, had great curiosity about insect biology, carefully reared out and collected specimens from our many collections for identification, and sorted out specimens from countless collections from Malaise traps. He was a patient and careful worker and made excellent mounts of pine tip moths and other Lepidoptera using a handy technique he devised. He participated in the Western Forest Insect Work Conference and he was respected by professional entomologists and other technicians in the Station and the Regions. When the Station closed the Shelterbelt Laboratory at Bottineau, Arden went to work for the North Dakota Forest Service in Bottineau as a protection specialist. His name appears as author or coauthor of several important publications.

Appendix D—Stephen A. Mata's
Recollections of the RM Station, 1964 to 2005

My working career started with a phone call from my high school Spanish teacher. One day as I was doing odd jobs with my friend Gilbert (to just get by), my Spanish teacher called me and said that he had a job for me. Little did I know that the call was to be the start of my career! His name was William Lopez. There's a school named after him in Fort Collins. That shows you what kind of man he was in the community. I really respected this man and so I went to see him. He handed me a phone number and a name and told me to go meet with this gentleman that worked for the Forest Service.

I remember the day I went in to meet this man. His name was Dr. Noel Wygant, an entomologist and project leader for the RM Station. He was a gentle man smoking a pipe. He talked softly and smiled, and laughed softly. He talked to me and Gilbert about careers in the Forest Service and told us that as time went on we would become valuable and advance in the future with the station. Boy, did he say a mouth full. I didn't know it at the time but this was to be the start of a 40-year career with the Forest Service.

Gilbert and I met with Dr. Wygant on Thursday and reported to work the following Monday, September 23, 1964 as forestry aids. Dr. Wygant introduced us to the scientist that we would be working for. His name was Melvin McKnight, an Entomologist researching the spruce budworm outbreaks on the San Isabel National Forest. My whole life took on a new meaning with this wonderful man. Mel was known by the name "Serenity," given to him by his peers. Mel was a soft spoken, gentle man that I believe was put in my path by my lord creator. Just think, I was at that age the military draft was taking young men into service. I was about to join the Army to complete my military service when I met Mel. Mel was a sergeant in the National Guard of Colorado. When I told him of my plan to join the Army for my two year duty, he sat me down and started to tell me about the advantages of joining the National Guard.

First and foremost, the military wouldn't draft me if I joined the National Guard. This would give me enough time to establish a temporary, probationary position with the Forest Service into a permanent position. So I joined the 180th signal battalion National Guard unit in 1964 located west of Fort Collins. I became a cryptographer in the message center section of my unit.

I started my long career with the Forest Service working for Mel. I attended a couple of introductory classes on insects at CSU. This started me on a long journey of insect research. I might say that I learned to crawl on the job with Mel.

William F. McCambridge, supervisor 2: After 3 or 4 years, other scientists at the station needed help with their studies, so Mel offered my services to William F. McCambridge, an entomologist who was to become my mentor. I advanced to the position of Biological Laboratory Aid and later to Biological Laboratory Technician. I learned many things from Mac, such as leadership, obedience, respect, loyalty, and much more. He was great to work for. I enjoyed about 17 years with him investigating the mountain pine beetle, a bark beetle that attacks and kills pine trees. When Mac first saw me, I was leaning up against the wall in a hallway. His first word to me when he passed by was "pitiful." For a long time afterwards the name stuck. We became very close. I've always known where I stood with Mac. When I did something right he would praise me by saying "Stevie, one gold star between the eyes" and when I would do something wrong he would say "Bend over and grab your right ear with your left hand and your left ear with your right hand and …." I could never do that exactly, but you get the picture. I loved doing things right for Mac. My head swelled so much working for Mac that I had to enter a room sideways. With Mac, I like to say that I learned to walk on the job.

John M. Schmid, supervisor 3: It was a sad time when Mac retired (1981). Again, I was fortunate to work with probably one of the most prolific scientists at the Rocky Mountain Station, John M. Schmid. Working for John, I earned a promotion and my title changed to Forest Research Technician. "Tiger," as I affectionately called him, was the man who was to become my role model. He probably would have conquered the world if he didn't have to contend with all that red tape. With John the mountain pine beetle research took on a different faze. We started to travel more and I would have to leave my family for a week at a time, sometimes for 10-day trips. These were the hard times. I didn't spend much time with my daughters growing up because we were always traveling. My sweet wife had to handle

USDA Forest Service Gen. Tech. Rep. RMRS-GTR-195. 2007

37

all the crises and heartaches. I would hear about them when I returned from a field trip. But this was part of the job I chose.

John had published many studies with beetles and other insects. I was very fortunate that he considered my work important enough to include me as co-author on many of his papers. With John's encouragement. I re-entered college to learn about the Fortran computer language. I also attended many class sessions given by the station's biometrician involving data summaries and analysis. As a result, I was able to analyze our field data so that John could publish at a more rapid rate. I spent about 10 to 12 years with John. With John I like to say that I learned to run on the job.

I enjoyed my 40 years with the Forest Service. It has been hard and rewarding work. I've had the pleasure of working alongside some of the best scientists in the United States and travel to many different states to do my work and to attend meetings. In those years, I was lucky enough to be added as co-author to over 40 publications. I'm most proud that we established thinning studies to combat beetle outbreaks. We also found ways to eradicate the beetle in infested logs using solar radiation and clear plastic, an environmentally safe method. I will miss the people I've come to know at the Rocky Mountain Research Station. I hope that it would be said of me that I always worked hard and respected the rules and regulations put forth by the Forest Service.

Appendix E — Daniel T. Jennings'
Recollections of the Albuquerque Lab, 1960 to 1976

In the fall of 1960, after completing a 6-month tour of duty with the U.S. Air Force Reserves, I was hired as a biological aid to assist John Chansler and other forest entomologists at the RM-Station laboratory in Albuquerque. Both John and I had served as summer field assistants at the headquarters laboratory in Fort Collins. The first summer (1958), John worked for Fred Knight while I worked for Roy Nagel. The second summer (1959), per Bill Wilford's direction, we exchanged supervisors "to broaden our experience." I spent both summers studying the Englemann spruce beetle on the Routt National Forest in northern Colorado. During the early 1960s, the RM entomological staff at the Albuquerque laboratory included Cal Massey, John Chansler, Eugene Ostmark, and Milton Stelzer. Ostmark departed shortly after my arrival to continue doctoral studies in Florida. He later signed on with the United Fruit Company in Central America. Bill McCambridge also served at the Albuquerque lab; however, he had transferred to Fort Collins by the time I arrived in 1960. During the early 1960s, RM-Station forest pathologists at the Albuquerque lab included Stuart Andrews, Paul Leightle, and Jerry Riffle. Prior to 1960, Forest Pathologist Frank Hawksworth may have served at the Albuquerque lab. Range Scientists Earl Aldon and Wayne Springfield were also part of the RM-Station staff but had offices on campus at the University of New Mexico. Later (mid- to late-1960s) they moved to the downtown location.

Initially, the Albuquerque laboratory was located in the basement of the main U.S. Post Office building on Gold Avenue between 4th and 5th streets. Later, the lab was moved to the 5th floor of the then "new" Federal Building, one block west of the Post Office. The lab and associated offices, including a library, insect museum, and photographic dark room, occupied most of the northwest portion of the floor of the new Federal Building. Sometime during the mid- to late-1960s a greenhouse was constructed on the roof of the Federal Building. It provided growing space for infective nematode studies. Additional offices off the northwest corridor of the new Federal Building were occupied by Region 3 Forest Entomologists Frank Yasinski (Yas), Don Pierce, and Don Lucht. Earlier, Al Rivas served some time as a Region 3 forest entomologist, but later transferred to timber management.

The early 1960s were tumultuous times following the split of forest insect surveys from research. As a result of this division, forest insect research suffered deep budget cuts, which unfortunately created some friction and animosity between research and pest control personnel. I recall hearing heated debates between Cal and Yas about this subject and suspect that Cal never fully recovered from the split. Nonetheless, the Albuquerque folks managed to move forward despite the ensuing awkwardness of a split team.

Coffee breaks were always a lively time at the Albuquerque laboratory. Cal Massey generally led the discussion no matter the subject. Who else could shout louder, longer, and with emphasized profanity than Cal Massey? We were kept in stitches most of time; however, we also respected Cal's vast knowledge of forest entomology and related subjects. He spoke with authority and from abundant experience learned chiefly "the hard way."

During my first tenure at the Albuquerque lab, I assisted John Chansler with studies on the cold-hardiness of *Ips confusus* and *Ips lecontei*. We collected "bolts" (sections of tree boles) of infected material from pinyon and Ponderosa pine hosts in Arizona, and transported the bolts to the Albuquerque lab where we waxed their cut ends with paraffin. We almost set the lab on fire one day when a pan of melted paraffin ignited! I also assisted Milt Stelzer with his studies on the Great Basin tent caterpillar (now Western tent caterpillar) in northern New Mexico. My "other duties as assigned" included pinning and labeling insects in the lab's insect museum. Apparently word had drifted down from Fort Collins that I enjoyed these curatorial activities. Cal often visited me in the museum and quickly answered any questions of insect identity. After my term appointment expired, plus an additional 30-day stint in the USAF Reserves (Hospital Laboratory Technician, Biggs AFB, El Paso), I entered graduate school at Los Angles State College (now University of California, Los Angeles) in the fall of 1961. However, I dropped out after only one semester, returned to Albuquerque, and signed on as Forest Pest Entomologist, with Region 3. Frank Yasinski was my immediate supervisor. During this time (1961 to 1963), the Carson and Santa Fe National Forests were heavily infested with the western spruce budworm which, in those days, was treated with DDT. Also during this

USDA Forest Service Gen. Tech. Rep. RMRS-GTR-195. 2007

39

time, Cal Massey continued to encourage me to return to graduate school, which I did in the fall of 1963 at the University of New Mexico. After two years of graduate work, I applied for a position in forest insect research and surprisingly was offered three (!) opportunities: at the Southern Station in Pineville, Louisiana (termites); the Intermountain Station in Ogden, UT (bark beetles); and the North Central Station in St. Paul, Minnesota (jack pine budworm). Cal Massey advised me to accept the NC Station position, and to continue graduate studies at the University of Minnesota. In Minnesota, I worked on population dynamics of the jack pine budworm with Harold Batzer from 1965 to 1968.

One day in the summer of 1968, I received a phone call from Cal Massey requesting that I return to the RM Station in Albuquerque and fill the position vacated by Milt Stelzer. Milt had recently transferred to the PNW Station in Corvallis, Oregon. Needless to say, I jumped at the opportunity to return to "the Land of Enchantment."

Shortly after my arrival back in Albuquerque in August, 1968, Cal once again "bore down on me" to continue graduate studies for the Ph.D. Fortunately, the Biology Department at the University of New Mexico accepted my application and dissertation proposal to investigate the life history and habits of the southwestern pine tip moth. Milt Stelzer had initiated some preliminary studies on the tip moth prior to my arrival back in Albuquerque. Field work began during the spring of 1969, followed by graduate courses in January 1970, and completion and defense of the dissertation in November 1972. Cal Massey served on the graduate committee; hence, I had no choice but to succeed.

As we all know, Cal Massey was a taxonomist par excellence. His pioneering studies of parasitic nematodes of bark beetles resulted in numerous new discoveries and descriptions of previously unknown taxa, including new genera and species. He achieved high acclaim in nematology with the publication of his magnum opus "Biology and Taxonomy of Nematode Parasites and Associates of Bark Beetles in the United States" in 1974. This published tome will remain a valued resource for nematologists, forest entomologists, and biocontrol experts for decades to come.

Cal spent hours, days, and years meticulously drawing and describing new nematode taxa. His pen and ink drawings on pebble board are masterpieces of scientific illustration, which I greatly admired. The nematode collection contains numerous holotypes and paratypes of new species.

To make a long story short, Cal Massey played a key role in motivating, guiding, and directing me into a research career with the USDA, Forest Service. Although he was tough as nails, boisterous and outrageous at times, he had a heart of gold. He was a good friend and mentor. I owe a great deal to him.

Sadly, I was the last research forest entomologist to be assigned to the Albuquerque lab. Shortly after Cal retired in 1972, his project on nematodes was abolished. Although I had been assigned to a separate project, and for a short time served as Acting Project Leader, it too was abolished and merged with Bob Steven's project in Fort Collins. However, I remained in the Albuquerque lab until January of 1976 when I was officially transferred to the Northeastern Station in Orono, ME, to work on spruce budworm. It was very difficult for me to witness and be affected by these closures. My departure represented the end of a long (1952 to 1976) tradition of forest insect research at the Albuquerque lab. The need for such a sustained research program has not diminished one iota! And, it is very doubtful that the "Big Bug Programs" will ever fill the void. In fact, such accelerated programs are probably responsible for the undermining of forest insect research nationwide.

www.ingramcontent.com/pod-product-compliance
Lightning Source LLC
Chambersburg PA
CBHW080620290526

45790CB00007B/2860